4TH EDITION

THE
PLAIN & SIMPLE
GUIDE
TO
MUSIC
PUBLISHING

BY RANDALL D. WIXEN

Hal Leonard Books
An imprint of Hal Leonard Corporation

ISBN 978-1-5400-6416-5

First edition published 2005. Second edition 2009. Third edition 2014.
Fourth edition 2019.

Published by Hal Leonard Corporation
7777 W. Bluemound Road
P.O. Box 13819
Milwaukee, WI 53213

Wixen, Randall D.
 The plain & simple guide to music publishing / by Randall D. Wixen. --
Fourth edition.
    pages cm
 Includes index.
 ISBN 978-1-5400-6416-5
1. Music publishing--United States. 2. Copyright--Music. 3. Music--
Economic aspects. I. Title. II. Title: Plain and simple guide to music
publishing.
 ML112.W58 2014
 070.5'7940973--dc23
                             2013045495
Printed in the U.S.A.

Fourth Edition

Visit Hal Leonard Online at **www.halleonard.com**

CONTENTS

ACKNOWLEDGMENTS

To Adam Holzman who, in the summer of 1967 at Tumbleweed Day Camp, actually knew the Doors and got me interested in the music business;

To my neighbor and friend George Braunstein, who was in the music business and let me work with him and his bands as I was growing up;

To Joe Nolte and Vitus Matare, who let me manage their band, the Last, and to the late Paula Pierce, who let me manage her group, the Pandoras;

To James Young from Styx, who believed in me and introduced me to Bernie Gudvi;

To Bernie Gudvi, who "brought me up to the majors";

To Tom Petty and Tony Dimitriades, for their friendship, support, and moral guidance throughout the years;

To Michael Jensen, who urged me to write this book, to Roger McNamee for giving me his detailed thoughts on the first draft manuscript and who continues to share insights with me on the music business and its new paradigms, and to Jeffrey Pepper Rodgers for his insightful comments and editing;

To my first son, Andrew Wixen, for his keen reading and comments on the second and third editions and for continuing on in the family business;

To Jason Rys, for his knowledge and insight, especially on newer technology and copyright law and for proofing some chapters to help ensure they were simultaneously accurate and plain and simple to the extent possible;

To Roy Sugihara for his kind offer to read and proof this fourth edition;

To Ben Davis for his watchful editing and being such a pleasure to work with.

To everyone else I've inadvertently omitted, who helped inspire me with their encouragement, discouragement, and/or ineptitude throughout the years;

To Sharon, who didn't want me to be an actuarial technician for PennCorp Financial even if it meant giving up that $1,270 a month salary, and who has become one of the stars of music publishing in her own right;

and to my amazing second son, Jonny . . .

Thank you all.

INTRODUCTION

Remember the story of the emperor's new clothes? It's a fable about a haughty and vain emperor who commissions some phony tailors to make some very expensive clothes for him. The swindlers charge the emperor a small fortune, deliver an empty hanger upon which, they say, hangs clothes that only the worthiest of people can see, and quickly make their way out of town. Rather than show that he is unworthy and cannot see what isn't there, the emperor puts on the imaginary new clothes and parades through the streets. Only a guile-free young child admits that there is nothing to see and remarks that the leader is, in fact, naked.

Well, the music business is full of naked emperors. I am continually amazed at the number of people I meet who hold the highest positions in the record and publishing industries yet know so little of the actual mechanics of the business. These people have attained their positions through force of personality, personal relationships, a little bit of knowledge, leveraging positions of trust, lateral moves from other businesses and firms, and various other (sometimes nefarious) means that don't constitute optimal qualification. It is truly rare that I meet people who actually know what they should know and are well qualified for the positions they hold.

With some frequency I get phone calls from managers of multiplatinum acts who want to know what a 3% producer's royalty means in dollars and cents, or from lawyers who want to know what normal industry terms are for various types of deals. Imagine negotiating multimillion-dollar deals knowing only that 4% is better than 3% but without a clue about the inner mechanics about how residuals are calculated.

I'm convinced that one manager I know is so dumb that he can only, and just barely, count to ten. So why is he so successful? I guess because whichever of his ten numbers he uses when negotiating a deal, he always remembers to authoritatively and convincingly speak it followed by the words "million dollars."

This kind of ignorance doesn't fly so well, though, in the current business environment of mergers, downsizing, copyright theft, and rapidly deployed new technologies like streaming. Those who actually know something (and sometimes, unfortunately, those who are simply cheaper naked emperors) are the ones who seem likely to be running tomorrow's music companies.

But what makes me so smart that I can judge my fellow industry "professionals" as being dumb and unworthy of their positions? Who decreed that I am the one who actually knows something? Am I just another guy who thinks he knows more than he does?

Actually I was pretty dumb when I first started out. I made a lot of mistakes and pretended I knew a lot more than I did. But after 40 years in this business, I've learned a lot of things through experience, education, and hard knocks.

I started my music business education in the middle and late 1970s while I was attending Palisades High School in Los Angeles. I worked after school and on the weekends for one of my parents' neighbors, who struck it big as a personal manager. I got to answer fan letters and fill out BMI forms. I didn't get paid, but I learned a lot and got to hang out backstage and in recording studios.

I started managing bands myself during high school and throughout college. But with personal management, I rapidly discovered that I was too Type A in this loose and creative world, often frustrated by clients who couldn't show up for that 4 p.m. interview or remember to pick up guitar strings before a gig. So I soon moved on to where I was most comfortable and useful, which was in the business aspects as the behind-the-scenes worker bee.

My formal educational background consists of a degree in economics from UCLA, where I was the music editor of *The Daily Bruin;* several professional postgraduate courses in the fine points of music publishing, song plugging, and international business law; and attendance at music business conventions, meetings, and seminars throughout the world. Locally, I attended meetings at the California Copyright Conference and the Association of Independent Music Publishers, among others.

For many years I have read voraciously on the subject of music business affairs and copyright law, both in periodicals and in books. One of my early first favorites was *This Business of Music* by M. William Krasilovsky and Sidney Shemel (Billboard Books), which I discovered on a shelf 40 years ago as a teenager while babysitting for an entertainment attorney's children, and which I devoured the way some kids devour comic books. More recently, the most current edition of Donald S. Passman's *All You Need to Know About the Music Business* (Simon & Schuster) is worthwhile.

Although I never went to law school, I've nonetheless been published by the local bar association, lectured at many law schools, and have often been asked to provide expert testimony in copyright cases. And while I never went to a business school or through an MBA program, I am frequently sought as a guest lecturer at trade associations and at major universities.

Today, I am the co-owner of a music publishing administration company based in the Los Angeles area (Calabasas) and a sister company in London (Primrose Hill). We employ 25 people who handle thousands of accounts, and our artist roster includes many of the top songwriters of the last 50 years. Our clientele and catalog is the envy of firms ten times our size. Our specialty is a highly detail-oriented approach to publishing administration, and we find and recover lots of unpaid and underpaid royalties every year. One attorney we know called us the "most anal-retentive group of people I have ever known," and we wear those words as a badge of pride.

So those are my credentials.

What finally pushed me over the edge and got me started on this book was a recent conversation with a singer-songwriter who has sold millions of records throughout the world. He kept talking about the mechanical royalties, and I assumed he knew what the term meant. But it ultimately came out that he thought, mistakenly, that mechanical royalties were his artist royalties. For five minutes we'd been talking about completely different things—the issue he was concerned about was not the same issue I was advising on.

This book was written, therefore, to put the necessary information out there in an easily absorbed form. I want to help musicians, songwriters, industry professionals, and even naked emperors acquire the knowledge that they want and really should have. I want this book to be a user-friendly, generalist's guide to music publishing, and not a comprehensively technical treatise on the subject. I want the book to be readable, interesting, and sometimes humorous—not just a dry dump of information. But I also want it to have enough depth that it is actually useful and not just an overview. I will try to keep the discussion and the examples simple enough that they are understandable to those who forget that 4 p.m. interview and their guitar strings, but with sufficient depth and detail to be useful to those either working in the music business or aspiring to be in it.

Almost everyone who has a career in the music business, especially artists who record their own songs, will tell you how important publishing is. Recording artists can run up huge debts to their labels for things like advances, tour support, recording costs, video costs, equipment, and the like. It is not uncommon for even highly successful artists to owe hundreds of thousands (even millions) of dollars to their labels over long periods of time. By contrast, publishing income is almost never recoupable from recording artist royalties and advances, so songs and publishing rights generate income that starts coming in as soon as the first time your song is streamed.

For many musicians, financial stability and an economically viable career are only possible via the songwriting and publishing income that is generated while their recording artist accounts are miserable bottomless pits. The adage "Don't give up your publishing" is as important and true today as it ever was. If you sell everything you've got, you don't have anything left to make money off of or sell. Most seasoned recording artists who write songs will tell you how keeping their publishing rights was the most important thing they ever did, or otherwise they'll tell you how selling their songs was the worst mistake they ever made. And songs have economic lives that extend way beyond the time when the single or album they were originally on disappears from the charts.

The subjects of music publishing, what publishers do, and how they should best do it contain many areas that are subject to personal opinions and preferences. My opinions are liberally interspersed with hard facts throughout the book, and I will do my best to be clear about which is which. I write as the owner of an independent music publishing administration firm and *not* from the perspective of a music rights licenser, a record company, or a publishing house that owns or co-owns copyrights. Ideologically, I believe that writers should retain their own copyrights and control them closely, and that alliances with multinational music publishing firms are rarely in the writers' best interests. You have been thus advised.

This, in fact, is now the fourth U.S. version of this book. So much has changed in the last few years that it is a bigger update than the previous three. For the first time in recent history, music is not prevailingly enjoyed by buying physical goods, but through streaming. Popular services like Spotify came onto the scene so fast, and became so big so quickly, that the business paradigms and copyright law had to play catch-up. Every time I thought it was time to do an update, something changed. Now with the passage of the Music Modernization Act in late 2018, it's time to explain the business as it currently exists.

My hope is that anything not covered in this book will be a fairly specific or detailed issue that requires expert consultation or in-depth research. If you make it through the book and absorb its contents, you might be missing a sock but you won't be naked anymore.

TOM PETTY
(A REMEMBRANCE)

Early in the morning of October 2, 2017, I received a phone call from Mary Klauzer, one of Tom Petty's managers, telling me that Tom had been taken to the hospital without a heartbeat and was on life support. I was told not to speak to any press that might call for a statement, and not to say anything at all to anyone until the life support was removed and until the family had made a public statement.

I endured the next 16 hours in a state of psychic pain and solitary pre-mourning. What I went through was nothing compared to what his wife Dana and his family went through. We were losing a beloved family member and one of the great songwriters of our time.

I first started working for Tom in the early 1980s when I discovered a $125,000 "error" made by MCA Records. When they messengered over a check to him for that $125,000 error, I became someone he looked to to cover his back end. He sent over a CD of *Damn The Torpedoes* that was signed "Randall, count every cent. Love, Tom."

Tom respected that I didn't try to become his best friend or part of his private life. He was just glad to have me there looking after his business. We'd speak or see each other a couple of times a year. He'd ask his lawyer or managers "what does Randall think about this?" from time to time because he knew I'd tell it to him straight.

Tom loved to make music with his friends even if it wasn't a paying gig, and many of the times I would see him was for one of these musical get-together parties. No original songs were ever played at these shindigs. Tom didn't want them to be private Heartbreakers shows. It was always greats by the greats played by friends for some friends. Stuff like "Carol" by Chuck Berry, "Green Onions" by Booker T. and the MGs, and reliably a few by John Lee Hooker.

One year, I was invited to his house for his 40th birthday party. A bunch of musical equipment was set up in the foyer. Eventually, Tom, Mike Campbell, Benmont Tench, Stan Lynch (sharing the drum kit with Jim Keltner), Jeff Lynne, Roger McGuinn, and Bruce Springsteen gravitated towards the instruments and started playing. It was mostly old blues standards like "Little Red Rooster" or "Mr. Tambourine Man"—since McGuinn was there (and since Springsteen always wanted to be a Byrd?). They weren't playing for the guests, they were playing for the love of playing with each other. There were many such musical get-togethers through the years including at a dive bar in Santa Monica (with Stevie Nicks and Bo Diddley sitting in), the Malibu Inn for his 50th birthday, Froggy's Restaurant in Topanga Canyon for his 60th birthday, and Mike Campbell's various New Year's parties.

Tom Petty with Stevie Nicks on tambourine. The cell phone picture was taken at the Heartbreaker's 30th Anniversary end-of-tour party at Harvelle's nightclub in Santa Monica. Bo Diddley also sat in with the band (his last show).

In February of 1992, I called Tom up and told him I had bought a Tom Petty model Rickenbacker 12-string guitar, and could I bring it over to his house and have him sign it for me. He said "Sure, come on over." I brought the guitar over (along with my 3 year-old son Andrew) and he took it out of the guitar case. He asked me how I liked the guitar and I begged off, saying I really wasn't much of a player.

He said, "You know, I told them I wanted the guitar neck thicker with cross-hatching on the edges, the strings further off the fret board, the pickups right here, and well, I'll be damned if they didn't do exactly what I asked. And it's the biggest piece of shit ever. I should be playing guitars, not designing them." We both laughed. In fact, it was one of the worst-selling signature model guitars that Rickenbacker ever made.

Roger McGuinn came to my office a year or two ago and saw the guitar on the wall behind the desk. I told him the story of Tom's disastrous foray into guitar design. He looked at the guitar and said it couldn't really be that bad. So we took it off the wall and Roger tuned it up and played "Mr. Tambourine Man" on it. When he finished, he looked up at me and said, "Yeah, it is that bad." And we laughed.

Tom had grown up in Gainesville, Florida, and didn't have a ton of money growing up. Whenever the conversation turned to money and someone mentioned an offer of "a million dollars," I'd watch him kind of go back in his head and he might say something like "You mean all I gotta do is play some guy's birthday party and I'll get *a million dollars*?" The momentary dreaminess would fade after a second, and he'd make a decision based on things other than money, but you could still see that *million dollar* possibility floating around his head. Principle always came before money, and he would never allow me to license any of his songs for advertising.

One year (before e-mail existed) I sent him a fax that said something like, "Tom, I just heard from Brad Smith (made up name) at J. Walter Thompson (the only ad agency I could think of) in Chicago, and he wants to do a McDonald's commercial with "Learning To Fly." The premise of the commercial would be new employees learning how to prepare menu items at McDonald's

Hamburger University. They'd be changing the lyrics to the song like this:

'We're learning to fry,
But we don't sell wings,
Selling Big Macs,
And the pleasure they brings.'

(I loved rhyming wings and brings....)

Anyway, Tom, I know you won't do advertising, but Brad said it would be over *a million dollars* and since it's your money and not mine, I thought I better ask you rather than just turning it down.

Let me know what you think."

Well, a few hours later, the phone rang and it was Tom. He said he had just received my fax, and was it really *a million dollars*?

I said, "Hey Tom, what's the date on that fax?" (It was April 1.) Tom said, "Oh, you're dead," and hung up. He dug it, actually, because no one else would try to pull something like that on him.

Roger McGuinn playing "Mr. Tambourine Man" on the Tom Petty model Rickenbacker guitar in 2015 in my office. "Yeah, it is that bad." Photo by Camilla McGuinn.

When I asked if he would write the forword for this book, he said yes without hesitation. A few days later, he faxed (!) it over in his own handwriting. God bless you, Tom.

FOREWORD

In the early '70s my bandmates and I arrived in Los Angeles, fresh and green, and within days of shopping our demo tape up and down Sunset Boulevard we were offered deals with three different big-time record labels. Just old enough to get ourselves into some real legal trouble, my pals and I went for the deal with the most money up front. A staggering $10,000. No small sum to us in those days, plus there was talk of buying us new amplifiers, and oh, first we had to sign something called a publishing agreement. This came up as we stood pen in hand around the desk, all set to close the deal of a lifetime.

We had no manager, which didn't seem to upset the label, who advised us we might need a lawyer to go over the contracts. We had found one with no trouble on the recommendation of a bass player we knew in Topanga Canyon. But publishing was something that hadn't really come up in our discussions. The lawyer had seen a quick thousand bucks and told us things looked good to him, so understandably there were some quiet stares between us as we sized up this deal-or-no-deal situation. Hell, why hold this thing up over publishing? Let 'em print the songbooks . . . So we all signed, and drinks were lifted.

Thirty years later, after throwing countless dollar bills at shaky lawyers, some of that deal still sticks to my feet. You may ask, "Who is he to complain?" and you might be right. It's true that after many a well-publicized lawsuit I was able to regain my publishing rights and have had a wonderful and lucrative career in music. But to this day I do not own the copyrights to my first few records. The record company went out of business, and through some spin of the wheel I wound up owning the actual master tapes. But the sacred publishing remains something that can't be bought. How could this happen? It's simple. I didn't have Randall Wixen's book! Hell, in the '50s, the writer of a book like this might have been dropped in a lake with concrete shoes.

Check the shelves: even today, you'll find precious little of this information made simple for the guy on the street. Why? Because music publishing is still one of the greatest scams for ripping off an artist ever created. I am far from alone in having to pay the price of an education in the music business.

You'd be hard pressed to find a songwriter without a similar tale of woe or one far worse. I once attended an ASCAP awards dinner and was fascinated to see, time after time, six people go up and take a bow for a song one guy wrote. To the man on the street it must be hard to imagine how something that is so personal and intangible can be wrestled away from the poor fellow who was humming something in his head, to become a stream of income for countless shysters, corporations, managers, and ex-wives. But yes, my friend, as you will read in these pages, this is often what happens.

It has been my pleasure to know this book's author for many a happy year of him managing my two publishing companies (as he does for a number of writers I have great respect for). And I always feel sure he'll track down every penny on B sides only released in Guam. Randall Wixen is that rare man of integrity in a business that I'm not gonna call crooked, but I'm not gonna call it anything else. Anyway, here's a chance to learn how to own those random inspirations that cross your mind, and a book that could be the most valuable writing partner you'll ever hook up with.

Enjoy,

Tom Petty

OVERVIEW

What is music publishing? Not what it sounds like. The term suggests the publishing and printing of sheet music, but in fact, this is only a very small part of what music publishers actually do.

Music publishing is the owning and exploiting of songs themselves in the form of musical copyrights. Music publishing is rights management. There are many types of *rights* within a *copyright* that can be exploited. One can license the reproduction of songs on sound recordings such as digital song files, CDs, and records. One can license public performance of a song. Songs may be *synchronized* in timed-relation with visual images in movies and television shows, in DVD and Blu-Ray disc programs, or streamed via services like Apple Music or Spotify. They can be incorporated into advertising, karaoke programs, telephone ringtones, samples, MIDI sequences, piano rolls, greeting cards, toys, video games, YouTube clips, Broadway shows, and more. And, of course, songs can also be exploited and sold as sheet music, both physically and electronically.

The music publisher controls all of these rights. Additionally, in almost all instances other than the licensing of sound recordings or the streaming of that recording embodying a publisher's song (where special *compulsory* provisions may apply), the publisher has the legal right to grant a license, or forego a license, for a particular use. In these instances, the publisher also gets the right to determine the license fee or royalty rate received through negotiations with the final user. In short, music publishers are really *rights holders* and *licensers* and not primarily people with printing presses.

The control and licensing of compositions is a unique responsibility. Great care must be taken to determine which uses are appropriate for a given song and what fees should be charged.

A long-term view must be incorporated into this analysis, and a particular license request must be weighed against the effects that the use will have on the song. For example, licensing a critically prestigious work to a television dog-food commercial for $100,000 would certainly make the publisher $100,000, but it would likely have negative long-term effects on other licenses and uses. Such a commercial, if well known and frequently shown, would in all likelihood make other artists less likely to make new recordings of the song and would also probably eliminate synchronization uses (i.e., the song in synchronism with pictures, as in films and TV shows). In other words, neither recording artists nor film and television producers would be as interested in using a song with strong dog-food associations in the mind of the general public. Accordingly, care in decision making results in the long-term health of a musical copyright.

COPYRIGHT BASICS

Under United States copyright law, a musical work is protected by law and inures to the benefit of the authors once it has been "fixed in a tangible medium from which it may be reproduced." This means once a writer records the work into a media from which it can be reproduced in his or her absence, it is copyrighted. Examples of this fixing would be writing down words and notes on a piece of paper, singing a melody and words into a laptop, or even developing a notation language and putting notches on a stick. The only requirement is that given the proper playback instructions or mechanisms, someone can reproduce the essence of your song.

The filing of a completed copyright form along with a copy of the work fixed in a *tangible medium* with the U.S. Copyright Office is a formality with many significant benefits. But the failure to do so does not mean that an author loses ownership of the copyright and the rights attendant thereto. Your copyright exists from the instant you "fix it" by putting it onto paper, on your computer, sticks, etc.

Registering your works does give you additional rights as a copyright owner. Registration is required, for example, before you can institute a copyright infringement suit in a federal court. Timely registration also allows you to recover statutory damages and attorney fees. But there is no time limit for registering a work after its creation. So if you wrote a song 25 years ago and never registered it with the Copyright Office, and someone just got a copy of it and put it in a film without your permission, you could presently register the song and then sue for infringement. But if your evil brother-in-law Smedley copyrighted the song 20 years ago without your knowledge, listing himself as the owner and writer, then you'd have a hard (but not necessarily impossible) time convincing a court that you are the rightful owner and claimant, and entitled to damages and other compensation from the film company.

Registration of a work constitutes *prima facie* evidence that you are the owner. Prima facie evidence is a little like a deed to your property registered with the county recorder. You might actually own the property, but registering the deed or your claim with the county gives official public notice to your claim. Such registration is pretty strong evidence that you make the claim to the property, but again, if someone wrongly registered a deed to your property in his own name with the local county recorder, you could still take legal action to show that such recordation was fraudulently made. Given the benefits versus the costs of recordation (both for deeds and copyrights), it is highly advisable to take this step.

Songs are registered in the U.S. Copyright Office on what is called a *PA copyright* form. PA stands for performing arts and includes not only musical works but dramatic works (such as scripts and videotaped improvisations), dance choreography, motion pictures, and other audiovisual works. (Before 1978, copyrights in songs were registered on E forms.) The charge for a PA copyright filed on paper is currently $85 and also requires that a deposit be made of the work as fixed in its tangible medium. A registration done via the eCO (electronic Copyright Office) system costs a much more reasonable $35 to register a single work. So you either send in some paper or do it online, (along with a file or CD of you singing your soon-to-be-hit song) and eventually the Copyright Office will send you back a copyright certificate with the Copyright Office seal on it. Because the eCO system is simpler, faster, and more streamlined, it is entirely possible that the copyright office will eventually stop accepting paper registrations. Note that mailing a copy of your work to yourself really doesn't offer any substantial protection or benefit. Spend the money on a real copyright application.

TWO TYPES OF COPYRIGHTS

An important distinction must be made at this point. There exists another type of copyright, an SR copyright, which is used to copyright sound recordings. According to the Copyright Office: "Sound recordings are 'works that result from the fixation of a series of musical, spoken, or other sounds, but not including the sounds accompanying a motion picture or other audiovisual work.' Common examples include recordings of music, drama, or lectures."

It is extremely important that you grasp the difference between PA and SR copyrights at this point, or the rest of this book will lack proper meaning. Let's take two scenarios.

You are the Beatles. (Congratulations on your fine career!) You have just recorded "Twist and Shout" by Phil Medley and Bert Russell. The music publishers of "Twist and Shout" own the PA copyright. That is, they own the composition itself. Your record label registers an SR copyright of you, the Beatles, doing the song. *This SR copyright does not cover the composition "Twist and Shout," but only your performing elements within this recording, such as your singing and playing of instruments.* The PA copyright in the underlying composition is still owned and controlled by Medley's and Russell's publishers.

Likewise, your contemporaries such as Tom Jones and the Isley Brothers, who are also recording this great song, have labels that are themselves obtaining SR copyrights for their artists' particular recordings of the song.

In general, then, there is only one PA copyright for the underlying composition, but there may be any number of SR copyrights corresponding to different master recordings. (In some cases multiple PA copyrights may be filed: for instance, for a work in its published and unpublished forms, or for [as examples] marching band and classical guitar arrangements of a song.)

So, Beatles, your record label now needs to pay for two sets of rights. The label has to pay the owners of the PA copyright for "Twist and Shout" for the use of their song on records publicly distributed, and it also has to pay for the right to embody the SR copyright master recording on those same records. In other words, the label must pay for the use of the underlying composition (PA), and they must pay you too for your singing and playing (SR). Copyrights in songs are shown as "© 2019 Joe Schmoe Music" and copyrights in sound recordings are shown as "℗ 2019 Rippemoff Records."

MECHANICAL ROYALTIES

The fee payable for the use of the underlying composition (the PA copyright) is called a mechanical royalty. The mechanical royalty is fixed at a statutory rate in the United States, that is, at a rate that is fixed by statute, or law. At the time of publication, the statutory rate for a song whose performance is under five minutes in length is 9.1¢ per copy distributed. Record companies have exerted lots of effort in lobbying to have the 9.1¢ rate changed to a percentage basis rate instead of a fixed rate for all sales. Currently, the 9.1¢ rate is what we call a "penny rate" because it is expressed as dollars, pennies, and fractions thereof. Record companies would very much like to have the rate vary as a percentage of some sort of arbitrary pricing, such as the retail or wholesale price of a record, and continue to lobby for such a change. The argument is why should they pay the same mechanical royalty for a recording that they sell for 35¢ as they would for one that sells for $1.99? The counter-arguments are that this would give them the ability to self-determine the royalty they must pay to use a composition, and further that it should be the song owner's right to determine what he wants to charge for the song rather than the company that wants to sell it.

Many foreign countries in fact base their mechanical royalty system on such a percentage basis. In general, publishers in the United States have been against this model. Whether the current penny-rate model will sustain or be changed in the future is something that will be hotly contested in any event.

The mechanical royalty that a publisher accepts may also be negotiated downward by the record company offering the publisher additional incentives such as advances. Such reductions are entirely a matter of negotiation between the publisher and mechanical user, and will be discussed at greater length in later chapters.

The fees payable to you mop tops by your label for your particular master recording (the SR copyright) are not governed by statute but by the terms of your negotiated recording agreement. These are generally called *artist royalties* but are on occasion referred to as *master license royalties* or *recording royalties*. For consistency's sake, we will refer to these payments in this book as artist royalties. (Mechanical royalties, too, are sometimes referred to as *copyright royalties*, but I prefer not to use this convention because, as explained above, there are different types of copyright royalties.) In general, the current practice is that artist royalties are paid based on a percentage of the wholesale or retail selling price of the recording, whether it is in CD, download, or other form. Or sometimes it is even based on sharing revenue (i.e., the label and artist might split the revenue equally after off-the-top costs.) Additionally, you as a recording artist may even elect to waive royalties altogether and do your recording for a flat fee or on a *work-for-hire* basis.

So we can see that both the songwriters and the recording artists get paid, and in separate and different ways. Now let's look at a second scenario.

You're still the Beatles, but now one of you has written a song called "Something." What changes? Not much really, except that you're now wearing two hats. You're the recording artist and you still get your artist royalties. But even though you've written the song yourself, your record label still has an obligation to pay mechanical royalties for the use of the underlying composition you've written. In this instance, such mechanical license and payment will be made to Beatle George Harrison's publishing company.

Recordings distributed via the Internet or otherwise in the form of electronic files such as MP3s or MP4s are treated in the same way. These distributions are licensed and paid for through what are often referred to as DPD (digital phono delivery) licenses. They are essentially mechanicals, but given a different name. Instead of being paid a mechanical royalty for a physical unit (a CD, for example), the publisher is paid a mechanical royalty for an electronic distribution (iTunes, for example.)

Subscription service uses such as by Spotify do not require a DPD license, and a full mechanical royalty is not payable. Streaming or subscription services allocate a percentage of their revenue to music publishers, less the amount, if any, they are required to pay to performing right societies. More about streaming will be discussed later in this book.

A few additional words of note on mechanical royalties. First, generally speaking, record labels must pay mechanical royalties to you for each and every record they distribute. Usual industry standard and practice is that no costs or advances are deducted from mechanical royalties, and that mechanical royalties are payable to you from the first record the label distributes onward. Artist royalties, on the other hand, are more typically recouped by the record label against the recording and other costs that it has advanced to you. For example, if the label gave you an advance of $25,000, the first $25,000 your record earns in artist royalties goes to pay back the label. Recording artists typically must earn back large balances before they start making money from a record, while publishers of songs on that same record are in the black from record one.

PERFORMANCE ROYALTIES

Let's move on now and discuss another type of publishing royalty, the performance royalty.

Performance royalties (and the underlying performance license) relate to the performance of your song in public. The performance of your song may be made in many ways and for many different types of benefits. The three most common types of public performance are performance of your song on radio, TV, or the Internet. Radio and TV stations and Internet sites like to perform your works because it helps them attract listeners and viewers, which in turn helps them to sell advertising.

Some other public performers of music (who must therefore license said rights) are restaurants, nightclubs, bars, aerobic studios, airlines with movie and/or TV services, kiddie gyms, schools, clothing boutiques, stores, telephone hold music services, elevator and environmental music providers, and concert venues. If you are performing someone's songs in public, with few exceptions, you have to pay for it.

Performance royalties may be licensed directly to a user by a publisher. However, the general practice of music publishers is to authorize an organization specializing in performing rights to license public performance of their works. The main organizations that license music performing rights in the United States are ASCAP, BMI and SESAC. Irving Azoff has also started a performing rights organization called GMR (Global Music Rights). These PRO's are not themselves publishers. Their function, and how they work to license and collect performing rights income for music publishers, will be discussed at greater length in a separate chapter.

SYNCHRONIZATION

Another significant source of income for music publishers is the synchronization fee or royalty. Synchronization occurs when a musical work is synchronized in timed, linear relation with visual images. Examples of this are background, theme, and featured uses of music in motion pictures and television shows. The producer or director might feel that music would enhance the impact of certain scenes or drama within the program. Pre-existing music is often licensed for this purpose and may include current hit or classic songs. Likewise, the producer or director might make arrangements with a composer to write music specifically for the production. Typically, pre-existing music is done on a license basis, while music specifically written to be a part of a production is done on a work-for-hire (or flat fee) basis, although there are occasional exceptions to these practices.

Just as we distinguished between artist royalties and mechanical royalties when discussing records earlier in this chapter, we must make similar distinctions here. A film producer requires two analogous sets of rights to put music in his film. First he must *clear* publishing rights from the publisher. Clearing publishing from the publisher (PA copyright) is also sometimes (more confusingly perhaps) referred to as a *sync* or *synchronization license*.

The film producer must also clear the right to use a particular master recording (SR copyright) within the film or, alternatively, create a master recording specifically for the film. To use our example from earlier in the chapter, the production must obtain a publishing sync license for "Twist and Shout" from Medley's and Russell's publishers, *and* it must obtain rights (a *master license*) to use a particular recording of the song. This master license might be for the master recording made by the Beatles, Tom Jones, or the Isley Brothers, or it may be explicitly commissioned and created by the production specifically for that film, and perhaps the corresponding soundtrack album. It is traditional, although by no means required, that such payments are made on a flat fee (as opposed to royalty) basis and that the publisher's sync fee is usually the same amount as the master license fee.

Synchronization licenses (except in rare instances discussed in the later chapter on synchronizations) may be declined by the publisher; for example, perhaps the publisher doesn't want the song in an X-rated movie or in *Rambo 13*. The publisher may also limit such licenses to a specific type of use (film festivals only, for example) or for a specific period of time (five years only, for example.) Likewise, the license may be incredibly far reaching, covering all uses within the program through "the Universe," for the entire life of copyright and any and all renewals, in corresponding advertising and promotions, on home video devices, and in any other media "now known or hereinafter devised." The range of synchronization licenses and terms is broad indeed.

Another important point to remember about synchronization licensing is that a synchronization use and a public performance are different things and involve different licenses and rights. Just because a producer licenses a song you have written to be synchronized with his TV show or film, it doesn't follow that a TV station or airline has the right to publicly perform your work for its financial (or other) benefit. Even though you allowed the producer to put your song in his sitcom, CBS TV must still obtain public performing rights for the broadcast of the program in which the song was synchronized. While this may seem like double-dipping, it really is not. It is simply the case of the two users of your music (the sitcom producer and the TV station) paying their own shares of the total rights needed for the broadcast. The producer needs only synchronization rights, and the TV station only needs the performance rights, so the producer does not obtain all rights needed to broadcast the show onto television sets everywhere but shifts this financial burden to its rightful place—the TV station. The producer gets no direct benefit from the TV broadcast, as he does not get to sell advertising for the broadcast, so he makes the TV stations pay for the public performing rights out of their advertising and other revenue. (An example of "other revenue" would be HBO, which earns money not from advertising but from monthly fees charged to end viewers.)

A final peculiarity of copyright law in the United States that bears mentioning is the fact that for TV and radio stations (so called "terrestrial" distribution because originally the distribution was done primarily through broadcast towers "over air"), we have no performance license or royalty payable to the owners of master recordings. So, if that sitcom that we were just talking about gets performed on TV, and if that sitcom embodies a pre-existing master recording, there will be no additional performing right fee paid to the owner of the master recording. While a publisher gets both a synchronization fee from a producer, and performing right royalties from ASCAP or BMI for the public performance of a song in a sitcom or other production, the master recording owner (unless the master was created as a work-for-hire) only receives a master license fee for the synchronization of the master recording and gets *no* performance royalty. (In many foreign countries, master performance royalties *are* payable. These master recording performing rights are called *neighboring rights*.)

This has become a hot-button issue in the U.S. music industry lately, especially given how much record sales have declined in recent years. Record companies are desperately seeking new sources of revenue to help them stay in business, and have pointed out how inherently unfair it is for the song to receive performance income, but not the master recording. Laws have been passed that have granted the right to receive royalties for master recordings performed via the Internet, Satellite radio, cable TV music channels, and the like. And it may well be the case in the near future that such performing royalties will be paid for master recordings performed in other media such as terrestrial radio and TV. (Although these aren't publishing rights, we will mention that most of these master recording royalties are collected by an organization called SoundExchange, and that the gross annual collections are now approaching $1 billion per year.)

OTHER TYPES OF INCOME

There are various other types of licensing and income for music publishers. While not typically as financially important to music publishers, these other licenses can, on occasion, be very significant. Within the printed music realm, such uses would include sheet music, matching album folios, lyric books, and Internet downloading of printed music. Karaoke uses and cellular telephone ringtones can generate supplemental licensing and revenue. The creation of a derivative work—for instance, the sampling or interpolation of musical elements from a pre-existing song, or foreign-language lyrics being set to an existing melody— may lead to additional use of a song. Video games, when successful, can be an important place where many songs are used and placed for profit (sometimes for a flat fee, and sometimes for a royalty per unit sold). And technology continues to advance at a pace where important uses of music of which we have not yet conceived may become commonplace before we know it.

SONGWRITERS AND PUBLISHERS

Up until now, except when you were busy being the Beatles, we've pretty much ignored the crucial element in music publishing: the creator of the song. Songwriters are often the most overlooked player in the whole process. You can talk business all day long, but if no one wrote the song, there is no mechanical license, no performing right, no synchronization, and no cellular ringtone. It all starts with the songwriter.

In the old days, and more or less up until the end of the Brill Building era in the 1960s, songwriters were rarely the same people who popularized the songs. Irving Berlin would write a song, and then Al Jolson would record and otherwise popularize it. Arthur

Crudup would write "That's Alright Mama," and then Elvis would have a hit with it.

In those days, a songwriter would affiliate with a music publisher, whose job was to get someone to record the song, or popularize it on Broadway or in a touring vaudeville show. The music publisher took a very active role in taking the song and then creating an economic value for it by doing what was then called *song plugging* (now frequently referred to as *professional* or *active* activity). The writer and the publisher were partners in the venture, and thus was born a traditional 50/50 split of income between the music publisher and the songwriter. The music publisher may have owned or controlled the song, but the writer got half of the money that the music publisher was able to collect from the users. (A slight exception to this generalization involving the treatment of performance income will be discussed in the later chapter on performance income.)

The true end of the traditional publisher/songwriter relationship and arrangement came with the advent of singers who wrote their own songs. Most notably, this was at the beginning of the 1960s when people like Bob Dylan and the Beatles started writing their own songs and putting them on their own records. Fingers started scratching heads as these artists wondered why it was necessary to split half the publishing money with a music publisher who was no longer fulfilling the traditional publisher role of getting the songs recorded and doing the work to make them popular. The new singer-songwriters were completing both functions (the writing and the popularizing) on their own and became reticent to receive only half of the proceeds for doing almost all of the work.

Many singer-songwriters moved to abandon the traditional relationship with music publishers and to start their own music publishing companies. With their own companies they could better control the use of their songs and keep a greater share of the income in a more proper balance to their efforts. Publishing administrators, and other people and companies with similar knowledge, would be paid relatively nominal fees to handle the business aspects of running the publishing company, issuing the licenses, and collecting the income. The songwriter, then, became both the writer and the publisher of the songs and retained the lion's share of the revenue and control, and it became much rarer for publishers to play their traditional role in plugging the music.

The traditional writer/publisher relationship still does exist and can be seen, albeit far less frequently, with artists who are not known primarily as songwriters (Barbra Streisand and Celine Dion, for example) and in quarters where the music producer (analogous to a film director) exerts greater influence, such as in the Nashville or hip hop and rap music scenes. Country artists still record many songs that they themselves have not written, although now the balance is shifting toward performers using their own material. Hip hop and rap artists often work collaboratively with a producer and an extended group of people to create a song.

This discussion of how the music publishing business has evolved resonates through the rest of this book. While the roles of writers and publishers has changed, the structure of the business as it was originally created still remains. To wit, the concept of splitting writer and publisher income on a 50/50 basis still exists in almost every area of the music publishing business. Even if you, Joe Schmoe, wrote a song and started your own music publishing company, Schmoe Songs, there is still the traditional splitting of income. ASCAP, BMI, SESAC, and GMR will pay half of the public performance income earned by your song to Joe Schmoe (the writer) and the remaining half to Schmoe Songs (the publisher). You are still receiving 100% of the income, but you are receiving it in two different pockets (two payments on two statements). This convention of a *writer half* and a *publisher half* persists and contributes to difficulty and confusion relevant to the collection, licensing, and allocation of royalties. Actually, if it weren't for such atavistic conventions, music publishing would be a lot less complicated and require less math and logic, and songwriters could do a lot more for themselves.

The intricacies and finer points of writer shares, publisher shares, and splits will be further explained in later chapters. The appendix lays out some mathematical examples as well.

DIGGING DEEPER

If you have absorbed the information in this chapter alone, you already know more about music publishing than many (most?) of the people you will deal with in the music business. The remaining chapters go into greater depth on many of the topics touched upon here (as well as others) and can be used for additional learning, research, or reinforcement.

THE VALUE OF MUSIC

This chapter is dedicated to Martin Cohen, who wasn't afraid to walk away from a deal if the money wasn't right.

This chapter is written as a subjective defense against those who devalue or undervalue music. Just as those who overvalue and overprice music have damaged the legitimate consumption of music and instead encouraged rampant theft, so too have some people in the music world damaged their own product by undervaluing and underpricing it.

Music is a unique commodity with the ability to touch the soul or evoke an emotion or feeling. In a film, it might take minutes of dialogue or visual exposition to create a mood or tell a story, while music can instantly convey a mood or direction and give cues to the director's vision. Try imagining *Apocalypse Now* without the Doors' "The End" or "Ride of the Valkyries," or *Casablanca* without "As Time Goes By." Typically, a feature film has at least 40 minutes of music of musical scoring. When was the last time you saw a film that had *no* musical score?

Likewise, some sports—figure skating, for instance—would not be possible without music. Imagine a college football game without a marching band. Restaurants and stores set the ambiance for you to be comfortable and buy merchandise by playing background music.

Yet in the music publishing industry, no day goes by without someone who recognizes the value that music brings to a project nonetheless belittles its value, complains about its cost, and tries to pay less than a fair fee. It is important that writers and publishers stand tall and recognize and respect the value of their own property. If they themselves fail to recognize the worth of their product, how can others be expected to see its worth and pay a reasonable price for it?

Today, many creators of music are finding it tough to make a living and are being forced into second jobs or alternate careers. It is so easy to listen to a song on YouTube, find a free ringtone on the Internet, or get the chords to your favorite song just by entering the song's title in a search engine. These services hide behind "safe harbor" provisions of the copyright law (which basically says that the web service has no liability or obligation to meaningfully police the infringing uses posted by its users), or are otherwise plain and willful infringers that would cost more to stop than the damage or theft is worth. "File sharing" sounds so much more innocuous than "willful copyright infringement," which, by the way, is a felony. If I steal your car, is that "ride sharing?" By spinning articles and headlines in this manner, the media contributes to the devaluation of songs and artists.

More and more people who used to just get by on low-budget music careers, maybe by playing a few sessions, putting out self-released CDs, and doing a two-month tour of small clubs or coffeehouses, are no longer able to do so. There are many who must now work in fast-food restaurants and other low-paying jobs. It's getting harder to eke out an existence and to buy time to develop one's musical craft. This is not a simple problem, with only one cause and one solution. While piracy and copyright theft each play an important role in this phenomenon, and while overpricing makes theft feel more justifiable, writers and publishers who lack enough self-respect to value their songs appropriately contribute to the problem.

When people started "sharing" song files that they "ripped" from CDs, or downloaded them from pirate web sites, it devalued music. The public expectation started to swing towards the expectation that music could be had for free, and this expectation of free or low cost music unfortunately spread to the community of other music users like TV shows and movies. Music creators and owners are constantly having to fight for the worth of their creations, and further too, many songwriters have unfortunately themselves bought into the idea that what they have done isn't worth much.

Perhaps nothing in popular culture demonstrates how lowly music is viewed by commercial users as the music credits of a major studio motion picture. Caterers, Second Best Boys, hairstylists, and personal assistant to the Foley editor's manicurist will typically be listed before the creator of the film's music after 80% of the film's audience has left the theater and the ushers are sweeping up popcorn to clean up for the next show. No animals were hurt during the making of this picture, but songwriters were.

"THIS IS A LOW-BUDGET PRODUCTION"

Almost every license request a music publisher receives includes somewhere in it the words "This is a low-budget [film/TV show/record/ad campaign/blah blah blah]." No one ever sends license requests that start off like: "This is a big-budget film, with two stars who are each getting 20 million dollars and a director who won the Academy Award for Best Picture last year. We would like to use the 'cherry' of your catalog and pay you a really nice fee for doing so." Or like this: "We have a multinational client who burned down half the Amazon rain forest last year and sold 300 million hamburgers and made 10 billion dollars in profit, and we would like to pay you some very significant money to use your song to glorify the destruction of the planet through cattle grazing." It just doesn't happen.

Why is the same company that is paying 4 million dollars for the network broadcast time of its 30 second Super Bowl spot balking at paying $250,000 to use your song for an entire year, and not just on the Super Bowl? Budgets are low because people set them low. If there is no money in the music budget of a TV show, it is because the money they put into catering, hairdressing, and makeup artists dwarfs the money allocated for music. Don't stand for it!

If you tried the same tactics in real life that are used in licensing music, you'd be laughed at. If you went into a Bentley dealership and said, "Gee, I sure like that $375,000 Azure, but I only have $30,000 to spend on a car, so do you think you could accept that?" you'd be shown the door along with some shoe leather. The idea that music has no intrinsic value leads to the proposal that "you should price your product according to our budget." Don't do it—especially if the song being inquired after is a standard, was a major hit, or has a lyrical or other connotation that is truly special. The situation may be different, though, if someone is inquiring about a generic punk song and the artist and song could be easily interchanged with many others.

"IT WILL BE GOOD EXPOSURE"

Once they get done telling you how low they've set their budget and how you have to conform to what they've predetermined, they will pull out the old "good exposure" argument. Or tell you that Bob Dylan and Bruce Springsteen gave them special deals. While the licensers themselves are only working for real dollars and maybe profit participation, they would like you to please take your compensation in the form of good exposure.

Vaudeville entertainer Sophie Tucker, so the story goes, was once offered a gig at far less than her normal fee. The reason she should do it, the argument went, was that it would be good exposure. "Exposure?" she is said to have replied. "Isn't that what you die from?"

The worst cases of "licensing by exposure" lately seem to be in the realm of video-game music licensing. With some of the "shoot the bad guy"–type video games now selling for $59.99 a pop and shipping 4 or 5 million units, you'd think they'd be able to spare more than $5,000 as a flat fee to license a song. Let's do some made-up math. Let's see, that's around $300 million in gross over-the-counter revenue, and maybe half filters back to the game developer. And paying $5,000 for each of 50 songs would be $250,000. And double that fee to clear the master recordings, so we're up to $500,000 out of the $150 million. It doesn't seem fair, does it, when music is so integral to the game? Why not at least pay a royalty instead of a flat fee? We're just now starting to see meaningful royalties on video games in lieu of flat one-time buyouts.

In the early days of video-game licensing it was typical to get a flat fee of $20,000 per song, and sometimes as much as $50,000 or more. Now, many of today's top young bands have bought into the good-exposure theory and license top nationally known songs for $2,000 to $5,000. Yet, as publishers, we don't see the results that all this good exposure will bring. We don't see a sudden surge (or even *any* surge, for that matter) when a hot new extreme sport game ships 2 million copies with your song blaring throughout various levels of the game and on the TV advertisements for it. It would be great to see some scientifically documented correlation between appearing in a video game and record sales, band awareness, tour ticket sales, or even public goodwill. Chances are, if the kid buying the game loves your song, he'll probably just stream it on YouTube or some other site where he can get it free, and what do you end up getting?

It's worth mentioning too, that with the number of mass shootings growing, some publishers and writers have taken a stance against "first-person shooter" games on the basis that these games desensitize people to shooting other people and creatures. And others just take the money.

Another example of licensing by exposure has entered the TV world lately in the form of *ad cards* or *chyrons*. The deal goes like this: If you let your song be used for a pittance, we will give you a two-second ad card at the end of the show stating, "Joe Schmoe's new record *Sing-along with Schmoe* is available on Schmoe-Tone Records at stores everywhere." Again, for these ad cards, it would be nice see some correlation or documentable benefits attained by foregoing a fair license fee.

A good way to weigh the "exposure" argument is to ask yourself a few questions. How unique is your song, and how special is it to the proposed use? For example, are they asking for a break on "You've Lost That Loving Feeling," which is an iconically unique song, or for a song your brother wrote that no one has ever heard yet called "I Like Playing in the Bathtub?" Is your song likely to be the best one for the use (Weezer's "Beverly Hills" to promote *Beverly Hills 90210* or Neil Young's "Ohio" in a documentary about the 1968 Democratic Convention), or are there lots of other songs that would generically work just as well? What will be the long-term effect on the fees you are able to realize for the use of your music if you give in and let a major studio use one of your songs for half of a normal fee? Is there any way to quantify or evaluate the worth of the exposure you will be getting? Will people even know it is your song being used?

Will they always want and expect similar pricing in the future? This is actually a serious issue. There are almost no secrets in Hollywood and any well-connected person can call in a favor and find out what an actor got to be in a movie or what a studio paid for the use of Al Green's "So Tired of Being Alone" in another film. It is hard to un-establish precedent.

Weighing these questions is a lot like playing poker with your own livelihood. If you always fold your hand, you'll never get any traction with a good hand. Likewise, if you always bluff, you'll lose credibility and they'll always take advantage of you in negotiation. Try to price your music fairly and in accordance with market norms, and to not give into the temptation to devalue your own assets.

A FOREIGN IDEA

One approach to valuing music is more common overseas than in the United States. That approach, used primarily in advertising at this point, is to assign a percent value to the music in a given campaign. Typically, this value is based on about 5% of the total cost of the advertising campaign. This 5% pool is then allocated to all the music being used in the project. If a $10 million European advertising campaign embodies your song, a $500,000 music licensing fee (half each to the publisher and master owner) would fall within current norms.

Such an approach is admirable in that it takes a bigger-picture look at the value of music, but it can skew unreasonably when the project it is being applied to has either a very big or very small total cost—or if the song is especially valuable or important. In those instances, subjective minimums and maximums within current norms should be applied.

Perhaps the reason that this approach is more common outside of the United States is that mechanical royalties in most countries are not based on *penny rates* (e.g., 9.1¢ per copy) but on percentages. For example, it would be typical that 8.3% of the dealer selling cost of a CD in a given territory might form an aggregate *mechanical royalty pool* according to local law or custom, and that pool is then allocated according to each publishers' number of songs or prorated aggregate playing time.

In any event, the percentage approach can provide a good alternative perspective as to what is fair and how music fits into a whole project.

STEP THIS WAY

Another approach to valuing a music license (usually involving motion pictures) is with what is called a step deal. Typically, an up-front flat fee is paid for a use. Then, if the film does well at the box office, on Netflix or Amazon Prime, or even in DVD and Blu-ray sales, there are bumps, or performance rewards. For example, a license might provide $5,000 up front, and then if/when a film hits milestones of $5 million, $10 million, $15 million, and $20 million, the producer pays the music publisher an additional $5,000 for each respective box office level.

The nice thing about this approach is that the producer is acknowledging the worth of the music, and even if he can't or won't pay you what it is worth now, he is willing to pay you a fair value, and maybe then some, if he has a success. The bad things about this approach are that you have skin in someone else's game and that too many step deals can overexpose a song for little or no money, and drive a paying user away from a song that has too much low-budget exposure and association.

SUBJECTIVE TENSE

You might conclude at this juncture that the pricing of music licenses is a difficult, subjective decision. Music is a unique commodity, and it has high intrinsic value that should not be discounted by either creators or licensers. There are many ways of looking at the value of music, and also many people who would like to pay you less than what it is worth on any reasonable scale.

Publishers and songwriters must both internalize and publicly exude the conviction that what they possess is valuable. Through education and through discussions with experienced industry professionals, fair win-win license fees can be determined.

It is often prudent, too, for songwriters and individually owned publishing companies not to handle their own negotiations. It is much harder to play poker and make the right decisions if your own money is on the table. If you are playing with your own money, you are more emotionally involved and less able to make the best-odds decision. Your representative will be able to take a more levelheaded approach. And please don't let someone convince you that it is your role to lobby your representatives to quote lower for the use of one of your songs. Rather, you should be telling them what a great deal they're getting, how much more reasonable the price is than you normally get, how much you desperately need the money (guilt is a fine motivator), and generally not working against your own interests.

Inevitably, and by definition, maintaining a license value results in fewer licenses. But doing so ensures that others know you attach an intrinsic value to a work. You might lose a certain percentage of the low-cost opportunities that are presented, but obtaining fair and reasonable quotes for the ones that do come to fruition will more than pay for the ones lost, and ensure the long-term value of a given song.

An example of this scenario is played out frequently by a music publisher who owns a very well-known song with a catch phrase that easily lends itself to advertising. In connection with the song, the publisher is approached for advertising campaigns every year or two. The publisher has priced the advertising use of the song in a one-year U.S. TV campaign at $500,000. When the publisher is offered $75,000, he declines it. While some may look at this as $75,000 foregone, he looks at it as $425,000 gained. For if the publisher had approved the $75,000 use, no other firm would want to run advertisements during that same time period with that same song. His experience has taught him that $500,000 is what advertisers are willing to pay for his song, and his experience has convinced him that there will be a significant use request every couple of years.

Unfortunately, some potential users will not be willing or able to pay a fair fee and they often will try and gain your participation by showing you footage and convincing you how cool their project is. But for the long-term health of the music, it is important not to devalue the song by licensing it for whatever a user offers. Bentley would go out of business if its dealers negotiated car sales that way, and so will you.

TYPES OF
PUBLISHING DEALS

There are many types of publishing deals. The most important variables in the various deals are ownership, administration, the period of time, and financial or "banking" considerations. The typical names given to different types of publishing agreements are determined by these variables.

OWNERSHIP VS. ADMINISTRATION

For our discussion, it is especially important to understand the difference between ownership and administration. A clear distinction can be made by analogy. Let's consider an apartment building called the Smedley Arms, located in beautiful downtown Douglasville. The owner of Smedley Arms is Adolph Smedley, who lives in Cannes, France. Locally, he has hired Simon Snott to manage the Smedley Arms.

Snott takes vacancy applications, screens potential residents, collects rent, chases down deadbeat tenants for back rent, pays taxes, does minor repairs, calls contractors for major repairs, pays the mortgage and insurance on the building, and generally oversees the property for Adolph Smedley. Smedley pays Snott 5% of the collected rents less monthly costs. At the end of the month, Snott balances the checkbook, prepares a statement, and sends the remaining profit to Smedley in the south of France.

In this example, Smedley is the owner and Snott is the administrator. Smedley has the ultimate responsibility for and ownership of the building, but Snott runs the enterprise on a day-to-day basis. Smedley has complete ownership of the property (maybe subject to a bank mortgage) while Snott has no equity whatsoever in the property.

If Snott is a good building manager, or administrator, then Smedley gets good and accurate accountings, prompt rent collections, careful attention to monthly costs, good long-term care, and care-free benefit of property ownership from half a world away. On the other hand, if Snott is an inattentive laggard, all sorts of things can go wrong. For example, if he does not paint over graffiti on the garage, the building will not look nice, and potential tenants will not want to rent the vacant units. If he does not take care of the cockroach infestation, other tenants will move out. And if Snott is a chain-smoking drunkard who watches soap operas all day long and forgets to keep track of who has paid the rent and who hasn't, Smedley will suffer. The same is true for publishing administration.

So now let's say Smedley realizes that his building is going to hell and flies back to Douglasville, only to find Snott passed out in a pool of his own vomit, running the building as a flophouse for transients. He immediately fires Snott and then personally restores the building to its prior state and starts interviewing new managers (administrators) so that he can return to his idle life in Cannes. He finally settles on Miss Lilly Logic, who has demanded and will receive 7.5% of the collected rents less monthly costs but is painstakingly reliable, with anal attention to detail. Smedley is obviously better off with Miss Lilly than with Simon Snott even though she charges a 50% higher fee for the job. The qualitative and subjective aspects of her work make hiring her an easy and smart decision for Smedley given the Snott alternative.

So, too, is it with publishing administration. Simply comparing percentages and ignoring the qualitative aspects of the administrators can be costly. The collections received by two publishers who each control half of a given song administered by two separate administrators each receiving a 10% administration fee will rarely be the same or even close. The income streams are almost always significantly different depending on the quality of the administration. Qualitative aspects include speed and accuracy of registrations and licensing, attention to detail, speed of accountings (how long they hold your money), and persistence in following through.

WORK FOR HIRE

As discussed in the "Copyright Basics" chapter, the most severe type of publishing deal is the work for hire. In a work-for-hire situation, you give up complete ownership and all administration rights for the life of the copyright. Legally speaking, too, you are not even recognized as the author or creator of the work. Compensation may be on a flat-fee basis, or the employer for hire may agree to pay you a portion or share of the proceeds.

Work-for-hire agreements are most common in film and television composing, where the studio wants to own and control the whole collaborative result and not have to keep checking with the owners of the incorporated elements. These agreements are also common in the advertising world for the creation of commercial jingles.

Typically, work-for-hire deals are for one-off projects and have finite creation requirements.

SONGWRITING

A songwriting deal usually refers to an arrangement whereby you agree to write a certain number of songs for someone else. The distinguishing feature here is that someone else will own and administer your songs, usually for a long time. You are induced to enter into this type of deal usually by a regular salary, payment, royalties, or advance against future royalties.

Songwriting deals are becoming more and more rare, but they still exist in certain areas of the music business. They are the nine-to-five jobs of songwriting within the music industry.

360 DEALS

In the last few years, we've seen the advent of something called a *360 deal,* which alludes to the 360 degrees of a circle. A 360 deal means that virtually everything is covered under the deal. In music terms, a 360 deal would typically cover your recording services, your publishing rights, your merchandising rights, your live performances, your acting services, endorsements, advertising, and just about everything else you can think of.

These 360 deals came about in a few different ways. Let's say you're Sally Superstar, and you're going to do a 120-date arena concert tour covering Europe, the Americas, and Asia. In the old days, your agent would negotiate something like 120 separate deals with the concert promoters in each city you were going to play in. Nowadays, Sally's agent is likely to sell all 120 dates that she is willing to play to a single promoter who is in effect buying the whole tour. This single promoter then sells off the dates in each market to individual venues, or self-promotes in some or all markets. What he hasn't paid or guaranteed to Sally, and what he hasn't paid out in costs, he keeps.

Some of these major concert promoters, such as Live Nation, started thinking it would be nice to expand the one-promoter concept to the one-everything concept. So, for example, Live Nation struck a reported $120 million deal with Madonna that supposedly covered not just her live performance services, but also her recording and other professional services. For the artist, the benefits of a deal like this are essentially a single business partner and usually a very large guarantee or advance. For the company, the argument goes that if they're promoting your shows, advertising your face all over the world, and helping you to sell your records by having you perform in front of millions of people around the world, why shouldn't they share in *all* of the spoils?

These 360 deals also came about in another manner, namely from the record company side. Labels were investing hundreds of thousands of dollars in signing new acts, developing their songs, crafting an image, publicizing and promoting the act, servicing radio and press, making videos, and oh . . . guess what? The record flopped, but there you are out on tour opening for Van Halen making $25,000 a night while the record company is $570,000 in the hole on your lame record that didn't sell. So record companies started to want to get in on your other action (i.e., the profitable action) and started making 360 deals of their own in which they participate in your live shows, your merchandising rights, and . . . your publishing (ten points if you guessed correctly).

In all cases, 360 deals serve to give the company a broader participation in all of your various sources of income. In return, the artists typically get more financial guarantees and advances and, in theory—because the company is more financially invested in making the act happen—more comprehensive career support and development.

If you're a big superstar and the 360 deal you're being offered is going to set you up for life, well, who's to argue? Just remember, once you and your posse pocket the megabucks, you've got nothing left to sell, so you better deal with your money very wisely so it doesn't run out on you. If you're a new band, a 360 deal might be the difference between getting $75,000 to record an album and buy some new equipment or the four of you getting $500,000 to put in your pocket to live on for the next three years so you can concentrate on your music without having to scoop ice cream for Tom Brady at J.P. Licks (a good employer, I'm sure).

Personally speaking, I'm a bit skeptical of the 360 concept as it seems to be driven by money and the people who are likely to commission your earnings, such as your manager, business manager, and attorney. The idea of getting a 15% commission on an advance that will cover virtually all of your professional income for the next few years is a pretty powerful financial motivation for a manager to get you into a deal that might not really be in your own best interest. The scenario tends to eliminate future career choices and locks you into long-term marriages with both the company itself and your commissioned representatives that may or may not work. You might decide that your manager is a loser, but he's already commissioned all your future earnings, so who else can you get to manage you now if there's nothing left for someone new to commission? Further, that record company to which you just forked over a cornucopia of rights might have a really crappy merchandising division and might be hiring some guy to start their "publishing division" next week.

Here's another way of looking at it. Let's say your pool man gets tired of showing up at your house every week, skimming leaves, and having your dog hump his leg while he's adjusting your pH for a measly $200 per month. So he offers you his 360 deal. For $1,000 per month, he'll also wash your car, mow your lawn, do your gardening, clean your windows, do your housekeeping, groom your dog, and change your air conditioning filters twice a year. You add up these expenses and realize that you're paying your pool man, gardener, carwash guy, housekeeper, A/C guy, and dog groomer $1,500 a month in all, so you'd be coming out $500 ahead each month. Might be good, except that he can't clean windows without leaving streaks, all your plants are dying, and your dog now has a Mohawk. While he may have been a very good pool guy, he wasn't very good at housekeeping, gardening, or grooming.

Which is a very long-winded way of saying: "Be careful!" In a 360 deal, you will be relying on your record company or concert promoter to handle your music publishing rights, and they might not be very good at it.

ADMINISTRATION

An administration deal offers more flexibility for the writer and the publisher. Ownership is retained by the writer or his designated publisher. The day-to-day handling of the music copyrights is the job of an administrator that the publisher has hired. Because of typical restrictions in an administration deal as to what the administrator can or cannot do without explicit approval from the owner, it provides ultimate control without myriad responsibilities. Typical administration fees are in the 10%–15% range, but as noted above, the qualitative aspects of administration are quite important, and administrators cannot be compared just on a fee or percentage basis. (Remember our friends Smedley, Snott, and Logic?) Administration deals do not typically involve advanced royalties or guaranteed payments.

Another advantage to an administration deal is that the period of time is variable and short when compared to life-of-copyright deals (work-for-hire and songwriting deals, for example). Typically, administration deals are two or three years in length. So if you end up hiring a bad administrator like Snott, your copyrights are not destined to be mishandled forever. You can simply take your catalog away from one administrator and hire another at the end of the term.

COPUBLISHING

A copublishing deal is a hybrid between a traditional songwriting agreement and something more akin to a simple administration deal. In a copublishing deal, ownership is traditionally (but not necessarily) shared on a 50%/50% basis. Administration is typically handled by the company to which you sell half of your song, on behalf of both the company's 50% interest and your 50% interest. The deals generally provide for ownership to continue for life of copyright, although in some instances there may be a reversion or legal limit to the length of assignment, allowing the original publisher (writer) to recover the assigned 50% interests in the copyrights or perhaps the administration rights to the 50% retained by the original writer/publisher after a period of time.

Because a transfer of both ownership and administration is involved, publishing companies are often willing to pay significant advances and guarantees as inducements for copublishing deals. Not only do these companies acquire the right to make money by providing administration services, but they also acquire some ownership equity in the asset itself, the song. They become both a Snott and half of a Smedley.

It is not hard for publishing companies to analyze and minimize the risk involved in offering copublishing deals. For example, a company offering a copublishing deal might investigate and determine that your first forthcoming CD has 12 songs on it that will each be paid at 9.1¢ each ($1.092 total), and that the record company will initially ship 75,000 copies backed by a $500,000 ad campaign, great press, and a video that is already airing on YouTube and has 25 million views. So if things proceed the way it looks like they will, your songs will likely earn $81,900 in mechanical royalties in just the few months after release, not to mention the streaming revenue.

If you are a new artist and a publisher offers you a $100,000 advance for a copublishing deal, this might seem like a huge amount of money, allowing you to buy your first car and put a down payment on a starter house. But remember that in this scenario, you have given away half the ownership of your copyrights and likely all of the administration rights for a long period of time, while the publishing company is essentially risking only the difference between the *recoupable* $100,000 it is giving you and the $81,900 that you will predictably earn, or $18,100. So the company has risked only $18,100 to acquire half of your copyrights on this album and possibly future albums for which you write the songs.

Much will be made of the fact that this results in a 75%/25% split in the writer's favor (remember, you still get the writer half and half of the publisher half as more fully explained in scenario 3 of the "Appendix: Can You Do The Splits?") to make a proposed deal seem more in your favor than in the favor of the publishing company to whom you have sold half of your songs. A copublishing deal does not obviate the need of the publishers to pay royalties to a songwriter under the traditional writer-half/publisher-half arrangement discussed in the "Overview" chapter. Therefore, a songwriter making a copublishing agreement can expect to have his account credited for 75% of the nonperformance income received by the company he has made the copublishing deal with (i.e., 100% of the writer's half plus 50% of the publisher's half, or 75% of the total). For performance income received by the company he has made the copublishing deal with, the split will be 50%/50%, or half of the publisher's share of the performance income. (Remember that you as the writer will receive the writer's half of performance income directly from your own performing rights society.)

Even if the numbers offered get bigger than our hypothetical $100,000 offer, there are some other important considerations to be given to a copublishing agreement. First, remember that the companies that are offering you the money are professional music-business bettors or handicappers of talent. If they consistently made back less in earnings than they handed out in advances, they would go out of business. So you may in fact be betting that you will earn less than these companies, which have a lot more experience in these matters than you do, think you will earn. In other words, you're betting *against* yourself with a professional bettor (that multinational music publishing company). Not only are these companies handicapping the likely success of your music, but they are covering their own overhead, the actual administration for your songs, the costs of advancing you the money, and their losses on writers who didn't make their money back for them.

Remember, too, that the money you are getting, while it might seem like a lot to e-mail Mom about (trying to justify your meager existence to your folks who think that it is still not too late to give up your music career and become a doctor), might be less than it appears. If you get $250,000, you might pay 15% to a manager, 5% to an accountant or business manager, and $20,000 to the lawyer for making the deal, leaving you with $181,875. Except that you will be paying half in taxes, leaving you with a net $90,937.50. This amount may or may not justify giving up half your ownership and all your control (administration) for a long period of time. You will have no future control over who collects your income or the quality of the administration they do. You have now cast your lot, and are just along for the ride.

Copublishing deals offer short-term, bird-in-the-hand money to writers, and they are also very popular with managers because they get an immediate payoff without having to wait for your career to actually develop and without actually having to work your record. If you're a flop, at least both of you got something up front. These deals effectively take some of your chips off of the table, cash you out, get you a partner, and spread the risk around. But they also hugely limit your upside and stick you into a long-term arrangement where you will have little or no direct control of your own work and have given up half of your ownership.

As an aside, if you look at the charts these days, you will probably find only a handful of the top 100 songs were written by only 1 or 2 writers. Some guy comes up with a beat, another guy goes "Ooooee Mama" every fourth measure, the producer says let's Auto-Tune the "Ooooe Mama" and loop it, and then samples two Van Halen songs, and suddenly there are 12 writers on the song. Publishing companies these days love to buy into the guys who are in the room these days and have 1/12 of everything that just went down. And they will promise that they can get you "into the room." They aren't buying into you as a competent and worthy songwriter, rather they're taking the mutual fund approach to song buying. Think about whether they're really interested in you or your songs, or whether it is really just to get another piece of the action. And frankly, you may not care, but just make sure you know what you're getting into.

Once in a while, if you're very lucky, the hype about you and your songwriting might be so great, and the money offered might be so emotionally out of proportion with reality, as to seem laughable. The music business occasionally sees ferocious bidding wars between corporate lemmings all convinced that their prognosis of your success is rational because all their competitive counterparts envision it too. When the money gets bid up into the "stupid" stratosphere, this is probably the best time to seriously consider these offers, although just where the stupid stratosphere begins is unfortunately subjective. Noncommissioned and nonpaid advisors are useful in helping you balance your excitement, impatience, desperation, and genuine needs against what you might be giving up.

There are other cases, too, when knowingly taking a sure thing (the money in a copublishing deal) as opposed to maintaining the future upside (holding onto your full copyrights) simply provides piece of mind, stability, or meets pressing financial needs. These bird-in-the-hand situations should be carefully considered and are very difficult decisions.

THE FINAL SOLUTION

Inevitably, there comes a time when songwriters, publishers, or heirs consider selling their songs (their catalog). To continue our apartment building analogy, song catalogs are sold in a very similar manner as investment real estate.

Apartment buildings are usually sold on the basis of the net amount of money they earn, or "throw off," per year. So too are publishing catalogs. Typically, a calculation is made of *net publisher's share,* or NPS. NPS is just like what it sounds like. It is the net amount that the publisher retains after paying writers, co-publishers, administrators, and costs.

Buyers and sellers of catalogs typically remove any extraordinary or not-likely-to-be-repeated activity from NPS. Examples of this might be if there was a sudden spike or nonrepeatable increase in income for a few months due to a writer's death, or if the song becomes the official Super Bowl theme in a given year. The nonextraordinary NPS for the last three (or possibly five) years is then averaged out. Sometimes an upward or downward trend is visible, but for most older catalogs, NPS will be more or less constant.

The average NPS is then multiplied by a mutually determined amount to arrive at a catalog sales price. Typical sales multiples these days are anywhere from 8 to 14 times NPS, depending on the prestige of the catalog, income trending, exploitation possibilities, and the situations of the buyers and sellers. So a catalog with a three-year annual average NPS of $100,000 per year might sell for $800,000 to $1.4 million.

A buyer can also analyze the expected rate of return by inverting the sales multiple. For example, a catalog that sells for a 12 times multiple has an annual rate of return to the buyer of 1/12th, or an 8.33% return on the investment. A catalog sale with an 8 times sales multiple represents a 1/8th annual return on investment, or 12.5%, while one with a 20 times sales multiple has a 5% return. (Of course, this is only if the NPS remains essentially constant.)

In valuing a catalog, care should also be taken to determine if and when the songs might be recoverable as discussed in the chapter "More On Copyright." If you are buying a catalog that only has three years left on the songs before the original writers are legally eligible to recover the songs, you would certainly want to heavily discount what you might be willing to pay. Correspondingly, if you are selling a catalog, you also want to take this factor into account in your pricing.

It is also crucial to examine the current tax status of a catalog sale. Over the past few years, there have been favorable tax laws and tax windows that have substantially lowered the tax you might expect to pay on the capital gain of your catalog sale. You should definitely check with a tax professional to find out the tax ramifications of a sale.

You should also ask yourself what the alternative benefit would be in selling your catalog. Let's say your catalog has thrown off $100,000 per year for the last ten years and someone offers you

$1.2 million to buy it. After you pay your lawyer and accountant for their work on the deal, and after you pay taxes, let's say you now have $900,000 left. What are you going to do with that $900,000? If you are going to invest it at 2.5% in a 5-year certificate of deposit, you'll return $22,500 per year. Obviously you were better off keeping the catalog that was throwing off $100,000 a year. Get good independent tax and investment advice!

However, don't forget that even if you are selling ownership to the copyrights, you still have the right to collect the writer royalties under the underlying agreements. If there are no underlying agreements, care should be taken to ensure the catalog sales agreement specifies that writer royalties are payable to the writers or heirs. Because NPS is calculated net of writers' royalties, the expectation of buyers is that they will still have to pay the writer's half to the writer or the writer's heirs. So even if you sell Dad's musical gems to some big corporation for millions of dollars, you still will have an ongoing income stream from the big corporation paying you Dad's writer royalties, but it will just be half of what it used to be. It is possible, too, to sell the writer's share to someone, but because writer's share is more like passive income and has no corresponding administration rights or control, it is more like buying or selling a passive annuity, and prices may be slightly discounted.

A great deal of caution should be taken in considering the sale of musical copyrights, and advice should be taken from someone quite knowledgeable in the field. Historically, musical copyrights throw off lots of money with little additional overhead. Income from musical copyrights, especially standards (songs that are recorded and licensed again and again), often rises, and thus so does the multiple value of NPS. Over the past 100 years, the value of significant music copyrights and the income they have produced make them among the best and steadiest investments one could have had. Their disposition should not be considered lightly. With the passage of the Music Modernization Act in 2018, it seems likely that both streaming income and performance rights income will be rising for the next decade or so, so a selling decision could be based on an asset that may be increasing in value.

BEWARE THE JABBERWOCK, MY SON

While we have talked about the importance of the qualitative aspects of publishing administration, it is equally important to disregard (or at least take with a big grain of salt) the intangible promises that will be made to you to get your signature on the dotted line. At some point in the process of trying to sign you to a publishing deal, most companies will trot out an extra-friendly person to love-bomb you and sell you on a fantastic vision of what they can and will do for you. No doubt, this person (the professional manager) will know every music supervisor in Hollywood, will tell you about all the songs that he or she has recently gotten into which film/commercial/CD, and is close personal friends with Producer X who is looking for songs for Superstar Y's new album. Or they'll promise to put you in the room with the guy who goes "Oooeee Mama" and the producer who loops and Auto-Tunes that, so you'll be in for a twelfth.

In the vast majority of instances, you will be shocked and awed into believing that this person *loves* your songs and *really* has the connections to do something for you. Be cynical here. I certainly am. Most big breaks happen organically because of your own talent and are not forced or suggested by a professional manager. If your songs are registered properly with ASCAP, BMI, SESAC or GMR as applicable, people will be able to contact you when they want to license your songs. Professional managers, in my opinion, are mostly there to field these calls that would come in anyway, though they try to give you the impression that they have generated the interest.

If this kind of professional activity worked as well as the managers would have you believe it does, then "professional" departments would be the largest departments at any publishing company. They are not. It is hard to find and hire professional managers who are truly able to generate enough new activity for a song or catalog that they not only earn back their own salary but make significant money for the company they work for (but they do exist). These genuinely effective people are extraordinarily rare in the music business. But "pretend" effective people are useful as window dressing to get you to believe that they will really do something for you if you sign up.

SONG PLUGGING

These people who promise to open doors for you sometimes make deals directly with songwriters and publishers that only have straight administration deals. They are known as song pluggers or sometimes sync agents and they offer to put their active and professional magic to work for you. Hiring one of these people to work on your behalf may be worthwhile, but with a few provisos.

First, the work that they do should be compensated by results they obtain. They should not get a fee, administration rights, or any copyright co-ownership for what they promise they will do. Any compensation or benefits they receive from you should be solely as reward for results they actually deliver.

A song plugger should not have the right to bind you to a deal or commit your song to a use without your approval. Many of the leads and offers that a typical song plugger turns up are of limited or dubious value. It is easy to find low-budget film and television producers who are just begging to find cheap music to fill their project while promising great exposure. A song plugger who wants a piece of your copyright because he got you a $500 film synchronization fee, which you only accepted because you didn't want to dampen his enthusiasm, will not be of any great benefit to you or your songs.

Where possible, it is far better to compensate song pluggers with a share of the income as opposed to a share of the ownership (equity) in your copyright. Give him a share of the rent; don't give away the building.

The best song pluggers are aggressive writers and publishers who actively network on their own behalf. The best song plugger I know is one of the most successful songwriters of the 20th century. Not a day goes by when she isn't calling a producer in the studio, having lunch with an A&R man, or calling a record company head. Even for those who don't have this kind of high-level access, there is always some place to start with polite and gentle networking—a bar where musicians hang out, recording studios and sessions, music seminars and meetings such as those sponsored by ASCAP or BMI, friends, or organizations like the Association of Independent Music Publishers, the National Music Publishers Association, or the California Copyright Conference.

Big-name artists and writers get writer's block all the time, and you'd be surprised how many would just love to coast on one of your great musical ideas. Approaching them with, "Hey, I've written a great chorus but I can't seem to finish the verses—can you take a listen and see if you could finish it up?" may be quite intriguing. Even if it is not and the door gets slammed in your face, the most successful pluggers, like the most successful salesmen, don't take it personally and simply go on to the next door. You are your own best champion.

A good plugger is not in it for the immediate placement or license of your work, but rather is geared towards making people aware of you and your songs. It is a long-term project to generate awareness, and even if you don't end up with a song in this or that particular film, the music supervisor or director is aware of you and your talent. It's a lot like "brand-building" in product marketing. Your expectations should be reasonable and long-term. This cuts both ways, though, because you might not know if you're getting the desired results for several years.

Finally, in recent years there have emerged several online music licensing websites. Typically, the sites offer to put your music on a site where potential users can listen to your songs and/or masters, and then obtain rights to use the songs at what are often stock, pre-determined fees for pre-determined rights and terms. This "trawling" approach to placement tends to attract users who need "stock" music at low prices, or to continue the fishing analogy, "bottom feeders." Besides the low fees generally realized, there is often the risk of not knowing how the songs actually might be used, and by whom. In terms of how these websites are compensated, all of the same concerns expressed earlier in this section with respect to pluggers should also be taken into account.

NO DEAL AT ALL

Another possibility is to make no publishing deal at all and do everything yourself. This can be done but requires a lot of self-educating. A reasonably intelligent person is certainly capable of figuring out how to correctly complete the appropriate copyright form. It also isn't that hard to join a performing rights society as both a writer and a publisher, and to register your songs. While paying close attention to the points raised in the mechanical licensing chapter, it is possible to issue your own mechanical licenses and not screw up too badly.

If you're self-administering your songs and, say, had an album that only came out in Japan, you could probably do some research, find a good Japanese subpublisher, and make a three-year subpublishing deal. But if the record comes out worldwide and you need to make and handle 15 or 20 subpublishing deals, you just might find yourself in the publishing business instead of the songwriting business.

I urge songwriters to try to do some of these things by themselves, or with the help of knowledgeable people, because the education, understanding, and frame of reference that you will derive from the process will be valuable once you get to the point of choosing between being a full-time publishing administrator or being a full-time songwriter. The most important characteristics for good self-administration are attention to detail, drive to completion, and relentless follow-up. If you don't have these characteristics, find someone who does. More about what is involved follow in the "DIY" chapter.

I HAVE IT HERE SOMEPLACE

Whatever type of publishing deal you make, make sure you keep a fully executed copy of the final deal in a safe place where you will never lose it. You should have in your own possession final copies of all the contracts and documents you ever sign. The tendency is to rely on lawyers, managers, or others to maintain these documents for you, but taking this one simple step will save you more time, money, and aggravation than you could ever conceive.

MECHANICAL LICENSES

Let's talk more about mechanical licenses and uses. If you did not read the "Overview" chapter and clearly comprehend what a mechanical license and royalty is, and how it differs from an artist royalty, you shouldn't be reading this chapter yet. If necessary, review the earlier material and then come back here when you're ready to absorb more detail.

Mechanical licenses cover many types of devices that can be used to reproduce music. Without limitation, a mechanical license can cover vinyl records, cassette tapes, eight-track tapes, DAT tapes, CDs, DVD-As, music files such as MP3 or MP4 recordings permanently delivered via the Internet, and even piano rolls and music boxes. These formats are generally lumped together under the name *phonorecords,* which in copyright law are defined as "material objects in which sounds, other than those accompanying a motion picture or other audiovisual work, are fixed by any method now known or later developed, and from which the sounds can be perceived, reproduced, or otherwise communicated, either directly or with the aid of a machine or device." Streaming is a unique hybrid, which is deemed to have two parts consisting of a mechanical license component and a public performance right.

Even though classical mechanical licenses and uses are diminishing in favor of new technologies such as subscription, cloud, and streaming services, they still remain vitally important to music publishers. There are always some people who are going to prefer the ownership model to an access model, and in most instances, the ownership model is going to provide higher sound quality and resolution over basic access models.

Hybrid formats that contain visual synchronizations or lyrics, however, do not constitute mechanical uses. For example, a karaoke disc that embodies visual images and has lyrics shown on a screen from which they may be read does not constitute a mechanical use.

Likewise, a DVD of a movie that features music as part of its soundtrack constitutes a synchronization and not a mechanical use. While such a use is sometimes referred to as a *video mechanical,* it has different legal properties as a derivative work and the publisher is under no obligation to grant such a license. A mechanical use must involve audio-only reproductions of music.

COMPULSORY LICENSES

The most basic type of mechanical license is called a compulsory license. A compulsory license allows anyone to manufacture and distribute phonorecords and/or DPDs of nondramatic musical works to the general public. There are several requirements that must be followed by the user. Of greatest importance, the musical work in question must have already been publicly distributed in the United States with the copyright owner's (music publisher's) consent. Once you have authorized public distribution of your song for the first time, anyone who wants to release and distribute your song may do so without your approval, provided he/she follows the compulsory license provisions of copyright law.

Let's look at this a little closer. Say you have written a song on the piano for your sister to tell her how much you love her. The only ones who have heard this are you and your sister. Can Bruno Mars, recognizing that you have written a sure-fire hit, get a compulsory license and release a record of your song? No! But what if you and your sister want to do a version of Michael Jackson's song "Beat It," which *was* commercially released and publicly distributed on Michael Jackson's *Thriller* album? Even though the two of you can't sing worth beans, and even though you want to do a heavy metal goth reggae version of the song that will have Michael turning in his grave, you can release it for public sale on your website and in stores! Provided that you don't change "the basic melody or fundamental character of the work," and that you are not adding new copyrightable material of your own (such as extra verses or different musical interludes), you only have to follow the compulsory license provisions of the copyright law in order to share your take on "Beat It" with the world.

COMPULSORY LICENSE REQUIREMENTS

So what are these compulsory license provisions that you have to follow so as not to run afoul of Mr. Jackson's publishers and his attorneys, who so detest heavy metal goth reggae music? Well, §201.18 through §201.20 of the U.S. copyright law tell you what to do. But rather than reproduce that spine-tingling prose here, I will summarize it. Of course, this is just an overview of what is involved, and you should really go to the actual law if you want to make sure you're in full compliance. (The U.S. Copyright Office makes a lot of summarizing pamphlets that it calls circulars available online at www.copyright.gov.)

First, you have to find the copyright owner (the music publisher) of the song. You can check with the Copyright Office to do this (www.ascap.com and www.bmi.com can also be useful), and there are provisions to follow that will allow you to proceed even if you can't find the copyright owner. With the passage of 2018's Music Modernization Act, the law specifies the funding (by digital streaming services), governance (by publishers and songwriters) and creation of a Mechanical Licensing Collective (MLC), which will also be a great place to locate accurate information about copyright owners and where to find them once it actually comes into existence.

For physical and digital file products, you have to serve the owner/publisher with an NOI, more fully known as a "Notice of Intention to Obtain a Compulsory License." Your friends at the Copyright Office can tell you how to do this by certified or registered mail, and you have to do this prior to or on the 30th day of your intended release. Of course, being a cheapskate, you will send this notice by certified mail since it is so much cheaper than registered mail.

If you don't bother to serve an NOI correctly and in a timely manner, you are precluded from ever obtaining a compulsory license. In other words, if you don't play by the rules, you don't get the compulsory benefits of the rules.

Finally, you have to pay Mr. Jackson's publisher the full statutory royalty rate. Currently, that rate is 9.1¢ for a recording under five minutes in length. Unfortunately, you and your sister made an excruciating recording that lasts for 9:12. So you have to pay the so-called *long-song rate,* which is currently 1.75¢ per minute or fraction thereof. (A nifty chart with the U.S. mechanical rates from 1909 through at least December 31, 2012, is reproduced here.)

United States Mechanical Rates

Date	Rate	Authority
1909–1977	2¢ per minute of playing time or fraction thereof, whichever is greater	Copyright Act of 1909
January 1, 1978	2 3/4¢ or .5¢	Copyright Act of 1976
January 1, 1981	4¢ or .75¢ per minute of playing time or fraction thereof, whichever is greater	1980 Mechanical Rate Adjustment Proceeding
January 1, 1983	4.25¢ or .8¢ per minute of playing time or fraction thereof, whichever is greater	1980 Mechanical Rate Adjustment Proceeding
July 1, 1984	4.5¢ or 9.1¢ per minute of playing time or fraction thereof, whichever is greater	1980 Mechanical Rate Adjustment Proceeding
January 1, 1986	5¢ or .95¢ per minute of playing time or fraction thereof, whichever is greater	1980 Mechanical Rate Adjustment Proceeding
January 1, 1988	5.25¢ or 1¢ per minute of playing time or fraction thereof, whichever is greater	1980 Mechanical Rate Adjustment Proceeding
January 1, 1990	5.7¢ or 1.1¢ per minute of playing time or fraction thereof, whichever is greater	1980 Mechanical Rate Adjustment Proceeding
January 1, 1992	6.25¢ or 1.2¢ per minute of playing time or fraction thereof, whichever is greater.	1980 Mechanical Rate Adjustment Proceeding
January 1, 1994	6.6¢ or 1.25¢ per minute of playing time or fraction thereof, whichever is greater	1980 Mechanical Rate Adjustment Proceeding
January 1, 1996	6.95¢ or 1.3¢ per minute of playing time or fraction thereof, whichever is greater	1980 Mechanical Rate Adjustment Proceeding
January 1, 1998	7.1¢ or 1.35¢ per minute of playing time or fraction thereof, whichever is greater	1980 Mechanical Rate Adjustment Proceeding
January 1, 2000	7.55¢ or 1.45¢ per minute of playing time or fraction thereof, whichever is greater.	1980 Mechanical Rate Adjustment Proceeding

January 1, 2002	8.0¢ or 1.55¢ per minute of playing time or fraction thereof, whichever is greater	1980 Mechanical Rate Adjustment Proceeding
January 1, 2004	9.1¢ or 1.65¢ per minute of playing time or fraction thereof, whichever is greater	1980 Mechanical Rate Adjustment Proceeding
January 1, 2006	9.1¢ or 1.75¢ per minute of playing time or fraction thereof, whichever is greater	1980 Mechanical Rate Adjustment Proceeding
October 2, 2008	9.1¢ or 1.75¢ per minute of playing time or fraction thereof, whichever is greater, plus 1.5% per month late charge	2008 Copyright Royalty Board Proceeding and still in effect as of at least December 31, 2012

Since you have 9 minutes and one fraction thereof (the 12 seconds), you have to pay Mr. Jackson's publisher ten times 1.75¢, or 17.5¢, per copy you make and distribute of your wretched little record. Hell, he should be paying you not to put it out!

The way that you have to account and pay to Mr. Jackson's publisher is, relatively speaking, onerous and difficult. Among other requirements, the compulsory license statements must be rendered on a monthly basis, and they must be signed and certified as truthful and accurate in very specific ways. There are also lots of other obnoxious hoops you have to jump through, so basically, no one really does mechanical licensing this way unless there's no alternative.

Compulsory licensing, and the types of uses that are available for compulsory licenses are intended to ease the burden of obtaining a license on music companies and services. In a non-compulsory licensing situation, the prospective licenser must approach the publisher, get permission, and negotiate terms. The publisher has the right to decline the use, or if the use is approved, dictate or negotiate terms. For types of uses for which compulsory licensing is available by law, there is no negotiation per se. Rather, the user must just comply with the notice, accounting, payment, and other terms that are provided by law. This makes certain types of licensing much easier because it is "automatic."

A ruling by the Copyright Royalty Board (CRB) in 2008 for the first time added a late fee of 1.5% per month to be paid to the publishers on compulsory licenses if the royalty payments were late. Since this is compounded monthly, this ends up being more than 18% per year and constitutes a very significant penalty to late payers. Obviously, the major labels were all up in arms about this. After all, why should there be a prescribed penalty for paying late or not at all? Writers and publishers are lucky to be paid at all, right? Negotiations subsequently took place between the National Music Publishers Association (NMPA) and the Recording Industry Association of America (RIAA), trade groups representing publishers and record companies respectively, who in 2009 reached what was referred to as the MOU (Memo of Understanding). Most of the major record companies agreed to be bound by it, and most major and many independent publishers agreed as well. With respect to compulsory licensing, the parties agreed to work together to improve mechanical licensing processes and encourage quick and accurate distribution practices for disputed earnings. The publishers agreed to waive the prescribed interest penalties provided that the bound record companies followed certain "best practices." Namely, the record companies actually had to try and license the songs, make certain prescribed efforts to find and pay the publishers, and had to distribute hundreds of millions of previously unpaid royalties to publishers that had never been paid.

Also as a result of the 2008 CRB ruling, digital product (same rates as physical product above), telephone ringtones (24¢), and interactive streaming (a percentage of revenues as a mechanical component payment) were added to the realm in which users could avail themselves of compulsory licensing. In 2012, additional types of compulsory licenses were announced and made available to music distribution companies and services. Those new license types and rates will be discussed in the "Streaming Section" which follows later in this book.

The CRB has hearings every five years to get input on what the various mechanical rates should be. They get input from all stakeholders, including creators and owners of music, as well as from record companies and streaming services. Then they make a ruling. In March of 2018, after a four-month trial that cost millions and millions of dollars in legal fees, the CRB ruled to increase royalty rates to songwriters and publishers by 43.8% for the years

2018 through 2022. The ruling also requires streaming services to pay 15.1% of their revenue for songs, up from 10.5%. This CRB determination was only the second meaningful rate increase to songwriters in 110 years.

Unfortunately, in March of 2019, Spotify and Amazon led an appeal that challenged this ruling, and now millions of additional dollars will have to be spent by songwriters and publishers defending the ruling against the appeal. NMPA President and CEO David Israelite made these comments about the appeal (which was on-going at publication):

"No amount of insincere and hollow public relations gestures such as throwing parties or buying billboards of congratulations or naming songwriters 'geniuses' can hide the fact that these big tech bullies do not respect or value the songwriters who make their businesses possible.

We thank Apple Music for accepting the CRB decision and continuing its practice of being a friend to songwriters. While Spotify and Amazon surely hope this will play out in a quiet appellate courtroom, every songwriter and every fan of music should stand up and take notice. We will fight with every available resource to protect the CRB's decision."

In a perfect world (for writers and publishers anyway), there would not even be a CRB determining how much publishers could charge for their songs. Publishers would like a flat amount per stream (such as 1/10th of 1¢ per stream or something) and not some variable "wave your hands in the air" nebulous formula based on how much money a streaming service charges or makes. How much a streaming service makes, and therefore how much it has to pay out, is self-manipulatable and self-determined. Headquarters in Little Rock, Arkansas vs. downtown Manhattan, executives flying first class instead of business or premium economy can make a huge difference to the bottom line. Self-determined advertising rates for the free tiers and monthly rates for the paid tiers can be priced low to build a subscriber base. Why should publishers subsidize this? Why should publishers' payments be tied to someone else's business model and desires.

Imagine if every five years a group of judges got together to determine what Chevy would be allowed to charge for each of its cars. Or if the price of a Big Mac was set by a royalty board for the next five years. It's kind of ludicrous that music has been singled out as the commodity that requires price regulation, and until the passage of the Music Modernization Act, the CRB judges weren't even allowed to consider free-market conditions when setting a rate. Thankfully, that has now changed. It's not yet a free market, but the judges can now consider willing buyer/willing seller arguments and conditions.

To be able to stream a copyrighted song on digital services, the Music Modernization Act made it so digital streaming services can get a blanket license covering ALL the music registered in the MLC. Getting a song by song license for a service that offers millions of songs was just impractical, and the forthcoming MLC will make it possible to get one license to allow them to stream every song listed in the MLC, and for publishers and songwriters to be accurately paid therefore.

Summarizing, then:

1. There probably shouldn't be a CRB at all, but at least now they can consider free market pricing and arguments.

2. Publishers and songwriters would like fixed rate per stream payments, but the digital services aren't going to agree to that any time soon;

3. The MLC will allow easier blankets for streaming services and better and more accurate payments for publishers.

4. Record labels and streaming services will continue to use efforts to minimize the amount that creators are paid.

MECHANICAL LICENSES IN THE REAL WORLD (FOR PHYSICAL AND DIGITAL COPIES)

In the real world, neither record companies nor publishers really want to deal with compulsory licenses. Record companies don't want to send publishers statements on a monthly basis, and, frankly speaking, most publishers don't want to get royalty statements to process every 30 days. On top of that, for reasons that you are free to guess, no one at any record company wants to hand-sign any statement that by law has to say "I certify that I have examined this Monthly Statement of Account and that all statements of fact contained herein are true, complete, and correct to the best of my knowledge, information, and belief, and are made in good faith."

So what to do? Well, the first step is still the same. You and your sister still have to find Mr. Jackson's publisher. But then, you *ask* them very nicely if you can please have a mechanical license. They could ask to listen to your and your sister's lousy version of "Beat It" and say, "Whoa, no, we're going to make you freaks go through compulsory license notices and provisions." Or they could say, "Hey, you're only making 100 copies of your CD, so it will cost us more to issue the license than the $17.50 we're going to be paid (100 copies times the 17.5¢ long-song rate), so you have to go through compulsory license notices and provisions."

However, in most cases, they will send you a license if you act professionally and provide them with a nice, neat (neatness counts) request telling them all the stuff they might want to know, such as: the name and address of your record label, the name of your group, the release date, the record number, phonorecord format(s) (e.g., CD, DPD, etc.), and the running time of your recording. Such license, typically, will provide that you only need to account to them and pay them on a quarterly basis, usually within 45 days of quarter end. In fact, though, the "mechanical licenses" that publishers send out are, when read carefully, not actual licenses, but waivers of compulsory license provisions to which the publisher agrees.

Specifically, the "mechanical license" will usually say something to the effect that we are waiving the requirement that we receive a "Notice of Intention to Obtain a Compulsory License," and we are waiving the requirement that you account to us every 30 days, and we are waiving the requirement that you hand-sign that horrible statement whereby you promise to be truthful and honest, and all you have to do is pay us every quarter, and gosh darn it you better be honest about it.

The Harry Fox Agency (www.harryfox.com) represents a lot of publishers and can often issue a pre-paid or limited number of copies mechanical license through its Songfile service. Other publishers and their representatives also may have similar services of their own. It is important that you go to the actual publisher or their authorized representative to obtain a license. Going to the Harry Fox Agency and trying to get a license for a song that they don't actually represent is no different than trying to get a mechanical license from your neighborhood McDonald's. If Harry Fox has nothing to do with the song or publisher you need, the delay in serving a proper NOI could preclude you from being eligible to get a compulsory license, so do your research carefully and timely if you need to obtain a mechanical license.

YOU'RE A PUBLISHER AGAIN

The U.S. copyright law, as discussed above, is very detailed about the requirements on mechanical licensing and accounting. In many cases, especially where an independent publisher is involved, a record company will only be too happy to prepare and submit a mechanical license for a publisher to sign, granting the record company the right to mechanically reproduce your (the publishing company's) song. You don't want to do this.

A mechanical license is not a mechanical license is not a mechanical license. If you only have the little knowledge that amounts to a "dangerous thing," the record company will take advantage of you (surprising, isn't it?). Here are some things that labels may try to get for their own benefit.

- They would like it if your license is not specific to a given recording artist or record number. That way, whenever in the future they want to use your song, they will not have to ask for a license, since your license is a *blanket license* that gives that label the right to use your song on any product or with any recording artist without the necessity of checking with you.

- They would like it if your license specifies a penny rate (e.g., 9.1¢) as opposed to being listed as statutory, so the license is not subject to any potential increases in the statutory rate in the future.

- Even if they do offer you a statutory rate, they may add several undesirable modifiers such as "minimum statutory rate" (which means that a long-song rate, where applicable, will not apply) or a "statutory rate as of the date hereof" (which means that even though they are paying you the statutory rate, it is fixed in time at "the date hereof" and is not subject to any future increase in that rate).

- They would like to pay you on the basis of records "manufactured and sold" or "manufactured, sold, and not returned" as opposed to what the Copyright Office and compulsory license provisions require of them as an accounting basis, which is "manufactured and distributed" (note that distributed records are not necessarily sold).

- They would like to have rate reductions for phonorecords sold/distributed at mid-line or budget price points, and they'd even like the rate waived for records they give away for free. (*Free goods* are, in record industry terminology, *not* records given away for promotional value. They are *bonus records* that are given to the retail outlets for free with each paid order. The retail outlets then *sell* the "free goods" to the general public. A typical record company "free goods" program might give the retail outlet an incentive along the lines that it pays for 85 CDs and gets an extra 15 CDs for free that it can also sell. In the absence of a good reason, music publishers should be—and frequently are—paid on all or some of the free goods. *Promotional records* such as those given to reviewers, journalists, and radio stations are, if within a reasonable number or percentage of total sales, typically exempted from payment of mechanical royalties because of music publishers' good nature. This need not be the case, though, due to the "manufactured and distributed" copyright law requirement.)

- They would like to pay you every six months instead of quarterly (or even monthly), and would like to pay you 60 or 90 days after the period end instead of the normal 45 days.

- They would like to pay you for only one "use" of a song per album. But what if your song is reprised on the album? Or what if a package contains three different mixes of your song?

- They would like to pay you at the same reduced mechanical rate (see following section) that you may have agreed to for physical product for their digital sales (see following section).

These are just *some* of the things you should look for. In short, mechanical licensing, while seemingly simple and straightforward, is fraught with difficulty and the potential for missteps. A music publisher should know what perils to avoid with mechanical licensing, because a simple, innocuous-looking one-page document can have serious deleterious long-term consequences.

In addition, there is one great weapon that record companies use to pay publishers less favorably than they would otherwise be entitled under the copyright law, and that is the *controlled composition clause*. These clauses are found in recording agreements and primarily affect recording artists who are also writers/publishers of their own material. The controlled composition clause, which will be discussed in greater detail in a later chapter, makes the recording artist guarantee that the record company will have many additional benefits with respect to mechanical (and even video) licensing. In some circumstances, legally speaking, a controlled composition clause can even be made to apply to music publishers and songwriters who are not even subject to or signatories to the applicable recording agreement. (The reasons for this horrible "I didn't sign it and I'm still legally bound by it?" situation concern nonexclusive licenses issued by co-publishers and are discussed in the chapter on co-writers and co-publishers.)

REDUCED RATE LICENSING

It is very common for music publishers to be approached by potential users who want to release phonorecords and pay less than the statutory rate. Most common is the three-quarter rate request where a record company states its desire to obtain a mechanical license at a rate equal to 75% of the statutory rate. If you went to your local gas station and gas was $4 a gallon, you'd have to give the proprietors a pretty good reason to sell you a tankful at $3 a gallon. Perhaps if you offered to have them tune up your car or if you bought a set of tires, they would see enough overall profit and let you have the gasoline at that reduced price.

Other than via a controlled composition clause (where a pre-existing reduced mechanical rate agreement already exists) the music publisher is in charge of the situation and needs some pretty good reasons to offer a 25% discount on a product. The most typical incentive given is an advance.

The record company will offer you an advance, frequently on a number of units, if you discount the mechanical rate by 25%. For example, if you agree to a three-quarter rate (i.e., you get 6.83¢ per unit instead of 9.1¢ per unit for a use less than five minutes), the company will pay you up front for 25,000 units (6.83¢ times 25,000 = $1,706.25). The advantages are that you are getting your money for the first 25,000 units in advance, and that if the record doesn't sell 25,000 units, you're ahead of the game. On the other hand, you've just waived $568.75 in income, and if the record does sell more than 25,000 units, you're in for a permanent long-term discount.

Typical unit advance offers for reduced mechanical licenses are 25,000 units and up. I have seen offers for 100,000 units, 500,000 units, and more. Obviously, the higher the unit advance, the more tempting the proposition. Likewise, offers much below 25,000 units provide, relatively speaking, very little incentive. A 15,000-unit advance represents just over $1,000 for a permanent 25% reduction in your income. It gets even worse when a publisher controls only part of a song. If a publisher controls 25% of a song that has four writers, a three-quarter rate for 15,000 units means giving up 25% of the mechanical income for around $250 up front.

By the way, there is no reason why reduced rate requests necessarily have to be on a 3/4 basis, and occasionally music publishers get 50% of statutory request or 87.5% of statutory, etc.

Another argument a record company will give for a reduced rate mechanical license is that it is a very small company and cannot afford a full rate. In other words, the company would like you to treat them charitably. Some publishers do, in fact, enjoy helping the little guy. Others find such requests disingenuous, as the smaller the company and the smaller the given release size, the less the difference in rate actually matters. If such record company is asking you to accept a 3/4 rate on a release with a 500-unit initial pressing, it is asking that instead of ultimately paying you $45.50 if all units manufactured are distributed, it will pay you $34.13, a savings to them of $11.38. In this case, the favor that you are doing for the little guy is so marginal, and the publisher's cost of interacting and/ or preparing a license doesn't change.

This brings up what, in my office, is referred to as the Law of Inverse Effort. There seems to be a pattern that when you're dealing with large amounts of money and very significant licenses, the deals get done much more quickly and easily than when you're dealing with small amounts of money and insignificant licenses (our 500-unit friend, for example), which seem to take a lifetime to finalize. The theorized reason for this is that those empowered to handle the bigger licenses have more experience and know-how, and understand industry practice and norms, while those working on the tiny little deals may not know the first thing about what they are trying to do, and can and will waste a great deal of your time.

As a music publisher, you could find yourself very frustrated with the little-guy label, who then brings in his brother-in-law, the personal injury attorney, to help close the deal, only frustrating you more because the guy doesn't know anything about copyright law or mechanical licenses but thinks he can handle it just because he is an attorney! Although well intentioned, the proverbial favor to the little guy could be the nightmare that never goes away in terms of your time and effort. So if you're the little-guy record company, please bear this rant in mind and remember that professionalism can and will be rewarded.

So, after all that, why grant a reduced-rate mechanical license? Sometimes you just wanna play ball. Most of the major record labels (including Warner, Sony/BMG, Universal/Capitol-EMI) have "special market" units that assemble and market compilation records (*Best of the '80s*, *Music for Lovers*, *Songs That Start with the Letter S*). If a publisher wants to have his music included on these various records, he may be inclined to participate in the reduced-rate racket. The thinking goes, "If I never approve the reduced-rate requests, they'll stop calling me and use some other publisher's songs on all their compilation albums. Especially since they don't *need* to use my song for this compilation and especially since there are lots of other songs that start with the letter *S*."

Another good reason to grant a reduced-rate mechanical license is if a song is a split copyright and your co-publisher or co-writer asks you to. You might not want to hold out for a full rate when your equal writing partner is only getting 3/4 for his half. Getting 25% more than a partner gets for his equal share, or even worse, making the co-writer or co-publisher pay the additional 25% to you out of their own pockets, is often awkward and thus a good reason to play along.

Reduced-rate licenses, finally, are frequently, but not always, granted on what is called a *most favored nations* basis, abbreviated as MFN. What that means is that the licenser is guaranteeing you the best deal that he is giving anyone. If he offers you a 75% rate on an MFN basis, and then later offers someone an 85% statutory rate, he will have to raise your rate to the "most favored" 85% rate. In this way, publishers tie their fate to other publishers and get a guarantee that they are getting the most favorable deal offered. A word of caution, too, is that the most favored nations provisions should apply to all material terms, not just mechanical licensing rates. Specifically, MFN terms should at least apply to both the amount or number of units of advance given *and* to the statutory rate of payment. You might not want to get a most favored nations advance and rate reduction when some people are foregoing the advance altogether and getting a full statutory rate.

It may be a justifiable policy, too, that with certain very important catalogs, writers, or songs, a music publisher will not under any circumstances grant a reduced-rate mechanical license. It all depends on what you're selling, and how valuable it is.

HARRY WHO?

In the United States there is a licensing organization known as the Harry Fox Agency. HFA was primarily known for issuing mechanical licenses (compulsory license provision waivers, as discussed above, actually). There once was an actual Harry Fox for whom the agency is named, but he died many years ago. In 2015, HFA was sold to the performing rights organization, SESAC. In 2017, SESAC (and thus HFA) was acquired by The Blackstone Group, a multi-national private equity firm.

For an 11.5% fee, the Harry Fox Agency will issue mechanical licenses on behalf of music publishers and perform associated and related services. Harry Fox controls the United States mechanical licensing on a large percent of the domestic music publishing repertoire, but not all of it. And because mechanical licensing and income has been greatly diminishing in recent years, they are now offering other services based on their knowledge, expertise, and proprietary data, such as processing and calculating royalties for third parties such as streaming services. I prefer to handle mechanical licensing directly for my own administration clients.

There are other, smaller, lesser-known mechanical licensing firms operating in the United States as well. In my opinion, there is no better alternative to direct mechanical licensing and collection between qualified music publishers and publishing administrators and the end user of the mechanical license. Communication and collection are thus direct between two principals without a third-party intermediary.

OH! CANADA!

Mechanical licensing in Canada can also be handled effectively directly between U.S. publishers and Canadian record companies. Many of the basic points are similar. Here are the prevailing Canadian mechanical royalty rates, expressed in Canadian dollars (at this writing, $1 Canadian is equal to approximately $.75 U.S.):

Canadian Mechanical Rates (in Canadian Currency)

1988 5.25¢/1.05¢ per minute
1990 5.9¢/1.18¢ per minute
1992 6.25¢/1.25¢ per minute
1994 6.47¢/1.294¢ per minute
1996 6.6¢/1.32¢ per minute
1998 7.1¢/1.42¢ per minute

2000	7.4¢/1.48¢ per minute
2002	7.7¢/1.54¢ per minute
2007	8.1¢/1.62¢ per minute
2010	8.3¢/1.66¢ per minute

As of 2019, the 8.3¢/1.66¢ rate is still the norm. The Canadians, though, have done something interesting. They abolished the statutory mechanical rate in 1988. Music publishers are thus free to negotiate and charge whatever they want to charge a Canadian record company for mechanical reproduction. Why then, are standardized mechanical rates shown in the chart?

The reason is that there is a Canadian licensing organization analogous to the Harry Fox Agency called the CMRRA (Canadian Musical Reproduction Rights Agency) that has negotiated a generally used rate. I generally use the CMRRA for mechanical licensing, and I also advocate its services for other types of Canadian licensing, specifically the Canadian Broadcast Mechanical Tariff (a mechanical-type fee charged to broadcasters for making duplicate copies of works) and the Canadian Blank Media Levy (a fee charged in Canada to manufacturers of blank media such as blank tapes and blank CD and DVD media under the assumption that at least some of the people buying this blank recording media are making copies of copyrighted material, and that there should therefore be a "tax" levied and paid to copyright proprietors such as music publishers). The CMRRA represents the majority of music publishers' songs in Canada, and on their behalf has negotiated mechanical licensing rates and terms with another Canadian organization, Music Canada (formerly CRIA, the Canadian Recording Industry Association), which represents the vast majority of Canadian record companies.

At the date of writing, the most recent mechanical licensing rates negotiated by the CMRRA and Music Canada, referred to as *schemes,* were agreed to and are shown in the previous chart. The rates given in the chart are not binding upon non-CMRRA publishers or non-Music Canada record companies, but these rates are "usual and customary" for the vast majority of music publishers and record companies and are used in almost all instances by companies not affiliated with either of those two trade organizations. But please remember, there is no *obligation* for a non-CMRRA publisher to accept these rates. The CMRRA-Music Canada scheme also makes provisions for other sorts of rates, limits, and even makes provisions for ignoring certain artist-controlled composition provisions (see chapter on controlled composition clauses).

Armed with the foregoing knowledge, it is not difficult for a U.S. music publisher to issue mechanical licenses to a Canadian record company. Many of the Canadian record companies will even (upon request) convert the Canadian dollar earnings into U.S. dollars and pay you in pre-converted funds. Due to NAFTA and other tax laws, there is generally no tax on Canadian royalties paid to a U.S. company. Unless Trump declares war on Canada or something.

Due to the Quebecois preference for French, Canadian record companies based in that province sometimes ask you to insert this or similar wording into a mechanical (or other) license agreement:

"The parties hereto hereby request that this license be drawn up in the English language. (Les parties aux présentes ont demandé que cette licence soit rédigée en langue anglais.)"

Go on, humor them. Canadians are nice people. Their population is relatively small compared to the U.S., but the country is an important music market. Canada has just over 10% of the U.S. population (325 million vs. 36 million), but the quality of their citizenry is high.

THOSE OTHER FOREIGNERS

How are mechanical royalties handled outside of the United States and Canada? Well for England, you can buy the UK version of this book, which is specific to the UK. Outside of the USA, Canada, and the UK, there are many countries that have their own rules, regulations, customs, and practices. It is simply not practical to discuss each country individually in these pages, so we will invent a generic foreign country and look at how mechanical licensing and royalties are handled.

The following scenario will apply for most countries of the world, with only the names, percentages, and royalty basis being changed.

Our country shall be called Forensia. Within Forensia, the government has set up an organization called FMS, the Forensia Mechanical Society. When a record company wishes to manufacture phonorecords within Forensia, it must pay FMS a royalty levy at the time of manufacture. The levy is analogous to a cigarette or alcohol tax in that the fee is paid by the manufacturer, who eventually passes it on to the consumer as part of the ultimate product cost.

In Forensia, the fee FMS charges is "9.009% of PPD." *PPD* is a real term meaning the *preferred price to dealers,* or the price that most record stores pay to the record company to buy the phonorecords. Coincidentally, according to the 12th edition of the NMPA *Income Survey,* 9.009% of PPD is the same percent charged in Austria, Belgium, Czech Republic, Denmark, Finland, France, Germany, Greece, Hungary, Iceland, Israel, Italy, Lithuania, Netherlands, Norway, Poland, Portugal, Romania, Slovak Republic, Spain, Sweden, and Switzerland, so this example is very typical. In some countries the royalty basis is based not on PPD but on adjusted retail price, an imputed (by estimate or agreement) or actual retail selling price, or some other basis. I know of no countries other than the United States and Canada that operate on a fixed currency rate per unit as opposed to some sort of percentage. In some territories the percent and basis are determined by government, by collective bargaining, or by another method. In Forensia, the amount and basis is determined by King Wastrel.

So King Wastrel has now decreed that all of the smaller (read: nontrustworthy or financially fragile) Forensian labels must pay a 9.009% levy on the given PPD to FMS before they can take their CDs out of the pressing plant or put them online and distribute and sell them. King Wastrel allows the major Forensian labels (because they are big and therefore honest and trustworthy) to pay their royalties to FMS on a monthly basis in arrears.

As you know, in Forensia, the PPD for CDs is 10.6 spazios. CDs are then marked up and sold in stores or online to consumers for 15.1 spazios. Doing the math, we see that when 9.009% is levied on 10.6 spazios, 95.495 spaziettes (100 spaziettes, of course, equal 1 spazio) are payable to publishers for each CD manufactured. FMS, our trusty local mechanical society, takes its 15% commission for overhead costs and local political bribes and kickbacks to the King, and then distributes the remaining 81.117 spaziettes to the various publishers whose songs are on the CD. In some instances, the local mechanical society distributes the collected revenue to the music publishers on the basis of the number of a publisher's songs on a given CD in relation to the total number of songs; in other territories, the revenue is distributed based on a proration of playing time.

The only other significant points worth mentioning about foreign mechanical licensing involve what is called *central licensing*. Central licensing means that, for example, Warner Records does not manufacture records in each country in a geographical area. In Europe, Warner doesn't manufacture the same CD in England, Germany, France, the Netherlands, Spain, Italy, and Scandinavia. That would be too much duplicate effort. Instead, Warner may manufacture all the CDs for Europe only in Germany, for instance, and then the German mechanical right society (GEMA) collects all the money for all of the CDs that will be sold throughout Europe. This is what is called "central" licensing, or in the case of Europe, "Pan-European" licensing. It can also apply to DPDs (i.e. iTunes and other digital copies).

GEMA distributes the net mechanical income available for distribution to music publishers to all of its sister mechanical right societies in the correct amounts relevant to where the total number of CDs are shipped. This system saves a lot of duplicated energy and function. However, it has also resulted in stupidly detrimental competition among mechanical right societies to lure record companies to manufacture in their territories and subject to their local rates. In other words, Society A offers a 9.1% PPD rate to a record company if it manufactures and centrally licenses within Society A's territory. Society B then bids down its beneficiaries' take-home pay (the mechanical royalty rate) by offering the record company an 8% of PPD rate. Obviously, this bidding war between different mechanical rights societies in order to maintain or grow their market share is not in the best interests of their clients, the music publishers.

Thankfully, in Forensia, King Wastrel kills anyone who underbids his mechanical rate.

WHO GETS THE MONEY?

Mechanical royalties are paid to the music publisher. The music publisher then pays the writer the traditional writer's half. If a songwriter also owns his own music publishing company, he can either write a check to himself as the songwriter or, if he is not keeping separate accounts or otherwise maintaining a distinction between the writer and publisher shares, he can just keep the money in one place.

PERFORMANCE INCOME

Performance income in the United States derives from radio, television and internet broadcast, closed-circuit and satellite music providers, nightclubs, gyms, concert halls, airplane entertainment services, and other places where music is publicly performed. Outside of the United States, the laws in many foreign territories provide for the payment of performance royalties for public performance of music in motion picture theaters.

Performance income may be collected directly by the music publisher from the broadcaster or end user (with a *direct performance license*), but in most cases it is collected by a *performing right society*. Performing right societies act to collectively license and distribute public performance income by means of blanket licenses. The United States is possibly unique in the world in that there are four performing right societies, ASCAP (American Society of Composers, Authors, and Publishers), BMI (Broadcast Music, Inc.), SESAC (which stands for the inaptly named Society of European Stage Actors and Composers), and GMR (Global Music Rights).

ASCAP and BMI are both nonprofit organizations that operate under court "consent decrees" and court supervision, so as not to run afoul of anti-trust, anti-competitive, or monopolistic behaviors. In many ways, though, this court supervision has put these two organizations at a significant disadvantage to SESAC and GMR, which as for-profit organizations are free to make whatever deals and charge whatever rates they want, without court approval. While SESAC and GMR are free to charge what they can get in the marketplace for their repertoires (for Pandora music service as an example) ASCAP and BMI are hog-tied with court rate-hearings and third party determinations as opposed to market-based determinations.

In most (if not all) other countries, there is only one performing right society, and it is often affiliated with the local mechanical royalty society. For example, in England, the mechanical society, MCPS (Mechanical Copyright Protection Society), has an alliance with the PRS (Performing Right Society). By contrast, JASRAC (Japanese Society for Rights of Authors, Composers, and Publishers) collects, licenses, and distributes mechanical, performance, and other income.

In 1914, shortly after the enactment of the United States Copyright Act of 1909, ASCAP was formed at a restaurant in New York City by a group of composers, authors, and publishers (including Irving Berlin) for the purpose of licensing public performance of copyrighted musical works. The society was, and continues to be, controlled by its own membership (approximately 670,000 authors, composers, and publishers according to its website) who elect the 24 directors.

By 1940, ASCAP was well established and, in fact, so successful at collecting performance royalties from radio stations that the stations themselves started a revolt of sorts. Some stations refused to play any ASCAP-licensed repertoire and would only play public domain material. Ultimately, the broadcasters formed their own competing performing right organization, BMI. Although owned by the broadcasters (this is a very significant difference between ASCAP and BMI), BMI operates as a nonprofit organization for the benefit of (according to its website) approximately 900,000 writers and publishers. Like ASCAP, it operates under a federal consent decree.

SESAC was started in 1930 by a German immigrant, Paul Heinecke, to collect royalties for what he felt were underrepresented European songwriters. The company is now owned by the private equity firm, Blackstone Group.

GMR was started in 2013 by Irving Azoff, and has mostly concentrated on very important songwriters and catalogs. Don't bet against Irving.

HOW THE SYSTEM WORKS

But enough of the history. How do performing right societies do their job?

Performing right societies generally operate using the concept of a blanket license. Radio and TV stations (and various other public performers of music) buy a blanket license from the performing right society. The cost of the license is usually based on gross revenue to the station and is typically around 2.5%. The more advertising the station sells, the more revenue the performing right societies get to collect. Given that there are more than 15,000 radio stations in the United States, the total amount collected in blanket license fees can be very substantial. That much said, terrestrial radio, as a media, has faced huge competition from the internet and satellite radio, and has had its fortunes decline in recent years.

What do the stations get in exchange for buying a blanket license? They get the right to play anything and everything in that performing right society's repertoire for a period of time. So if a radio station buys blanket licenses from ASCAP, BMI, SESAC and GMR, it can play virtually every published song. This is far easier for the stations than contacting each publisher individually and getting the direct right and license from that publisher to perform its song on the radio. Likewise, the blanket license concept is far easier for music publishers, who don't have to issue licenses to 15,000 radio stations and other public performers of music.

Each of the performing right societies negotiate the cost of blanket licenses based on arguments they make on the relative importance of their repertoire and the percentage of a user's total performance time this repertoire accounts for. For example, ASCAP might tell a given radio station, "Look, last year ASCAP music comprised 43% of the music you broadcast, whereas in the previous year, ASCAP music only made up 39%, so we should get more money for our license this year." Likewise, SESAC might inform a TV station, "We now represent the repertoires of Neil Diamond and Bob Dylan, so you need to pay us a lot more than you did before."

Of lesser importance than the blanket license concept is the *per-program* license. Public performers of music who use little or no music, or who have special agendas or needs, may seek to avail themselves of per-program licensing. For example, talk radio and news stations make very little of their revenue from playing music that people want to hear; instead they rely on interesting (?) talk hosts and stories. It might be more prudent to pay only for the exact music they play, each and every time they play it, than to buy a blanket license. Small, independent TV stations would also be good candidates for per-program licenses.

DIRECT LICENSES

Some public performers of music simply refuse to get either blanket or per-program licenses from the performing right societies. In these cases, they actually seek out the original music publishers and negotiate a public performance license directly. ESPN, for instance, likes to obtain public performance licenses directly from publishers and, if the license is not easily obtained, gets a per-program license from the applicable society. The Weather Channel can easily control its musical content and, as of this writing, does not obtain blanket performing right licenses.

Under the terms of the applicable consent decrees under which ASCAP and BMI operate, ASCAP and BMI only obtain *nonexclusive* performing rights to a publisher's repertoire. This means that a publisher also retains the right to issue public performance licenses even though its performing right society represents that same repertoire. The only caveat is that if publishers license a work directly for public performance, they need to tell their performing right societies that they have done this. The reason for this is to prevent a performing right society from instituting a lawsuit against a party for public performance without a license when in fact the user obtained such license directly from the publisher.

Recently, some publishers have tried to withdraw certain categories of rights (internet streaming for example) from the rights they have given ASCAP or BMI so that they may directly negotiate market rates for the use of their music as opposed to having such rates being court determined under the consent decrees. The courts have so far knocked this down. This fragmentary approach to rights could be detrimental to the strength of organizations like ASCAP and BMI.

OK, SO WHERE DOES ALL THE MONEY GO?

ASCAP, BMI, SESAC, and GMR collectively bring in enormous sums of money from blanket and performance licenses that go into giant funds. From the fund of each organization, operating expenses are deducted, and the remaining sums are distributed to the songwriters and publishers. In the cases of SESAC and GMR, there is also a profit component, which may be deducted. To give you some actual numbers, in 2018 ASCAP's collections were $1.227 billion, of which $1.109 billion was distributed to members. BMI's gross collections for its fiscal year 2018 were announced at $1.199 billion with distributions of $1.118 billion.

GETTING IN ON THE ACTION

Music publishers and songwriters can join ASCAP, BMI, SESAC, or GMR. There are separate performing right society affiliations, and separate agreements, for music publishers and songwriters. Songwriters can only join one United States performing right society, and their affiliation with that society is exclusive. Songwriters are free to move between one society or another upon the expiration of their affiliation term. (In some instances, a BMI writer may elect to leave certain specific works to be licensed by BMI after he has terminated his BMI affiliation and joined ASCAP, but he will still be considered a current ASCAP writer even though prior repertoire remains with and is licensed by BMI.)

Publishers, because they may publish works written by ASCAP, BMI, SESAC, and GMR songwriters, typically have publishing companies affiliated with two or even three performing right societies. In rare instances, a writer may join one performing right society for the United States and then have a different performing right society represent him for the rest of the world. This might be done, for instance, by a film composer who, while a citizen and resident of Germany, derives a lot of public performance from United States broadcasts and wishes to avail himself of the benefits of direct membership, statements, and payments. Sometimes, too, signing with different societies for U.S. and overseas performing rights is done for tax reasons: to keep otherwise taxable income out of the country of residence.

Here are some specific points to remember with respect to performing right societies.

- A publisher's affiliation on a given work must be the same as a writer's affiliation. For example, an ASCAP publisher cannot publish a BMI writer's work, and a BMI publisher cannot publish an ASCAP writer's work.

- If a song is co-written by songwriters with differing affiliations, the proportion of affiliation must remain with respect to publishing. If one ASCAP songwriter writes 20% of a song, and two BMI writers each wrote 40% of that same song, the song must be published 20% by an ASCAP company and 80% by BMI companies. (Foreign writers and publishers who are not members of BMI, ASCAP, or SESAC are free to designate which U.S. performing right society will license and collect revenue on a song-by-song basis. In other words, some titles can be licensed through BMI and some through ASCAP, SESAC, or GMR.)

- The United States performing right societies have reciprocal agreements with their counterparts in other countries. So if you are a member of, say, ASCAP, ASCAP will register your songs internationally for public performance licensing, and ASCAP's sister societies overseas will collect your performing right income and pay it to ASCAP, which will then pay it to you. You do not need to join performing right societies all over the world.

- Performing rights income is handled differently than almost any other type of music publishing income. The difference is that the performing right society splits the money due for a song's public performance, paying the writer half *directly* to the writer and paying the publisher's half *directly* to the publisher. If you are not clear on writer's half and publisher's half, please reread "Songwriters and Publishers" in the "Overview" chapter. Take a moment to absorb this. Unlike mechanical royalties, where the publisher gets everything and pays half to the writer, ASCAP, BMI, SESAC, and GMR think your publisher is untrustworthy scum (he just might be) and want you to receive your half directly before he can get his grubby little hands on it. Accordingly, if you are a self-published writer, you will get two separate (and mostly equal) accountings for the same performances from your performing right society: one for the writer share (Joe Schmoe) and one for the publisher share (Schmoe Songs). They are not double paying you. (You wish.)

For this reason, income splits are often different for different types of publishing revenue. You might be entitled to 50% of mechanical and synchronization income from your publisher, but entitled to 0% of the public performance income the publisher receives because (ten points if you guessed it) you received your half of the public performance income directly from your performing right society.

- ASCAP lives in a 100% world. This means that for a given song, every participant on an ASCAP song adds up to 100%. Broken down further, the "publisher shares" on ASCAP repertoire equal 50%, and the writer shares correspondingly add up to a total of 50%, so that the gross total paid out is reflected as 100%. BMI, on the other hand, lives in a 200% world (except for works in the specified format known as CWR [common works registration]). The publisher shares add up to 100% of "publisher share" and the writer shares also add up to 100% of "writer share." Obviously, BMI doesn't pay out double what it owes, so this is really just a convenient, albeit confusing, convention. The reason for this could be because they don't want to get phone calls from guys who say, "Hey, I wrote 100% of this song, how come the statement you sent shows that I'm only getting 50%?"

To try to make it even more complicated, our foreign friends sometimes use two different conventions to designate splits for performance and other types of income. If you are a 100% publisher of a song, you would get 100% of the mechanical and other income and 100% of the (publisher's share of) performance income in the

United States. Frequently, though, foreign right societies (JASRAC in Japan for example) express performing income as a fraction, usually with a denominator of 12. So in the case of Japan, you as a 100% publisher would claim 100% of mechanical and other income, and 6/12 of the performance income. The 6/12 is supposed to make it easier and remind you that this is performance income and that you are only getting half of the whole. In other words, 6/12 is 100% of the publisher's share of performance income. If these conventions further confuse you, just keep telling yourself that they make life easier.

I STILL HAVEN'T BEEN PAID

OK, so ASCAP has a half a billion dollars sitting in a bank somewhere and you want your share. You've joined ASCAP as a writer and as a publisher, and you want your money already. How do the performing right societies figure out how much of the blanket and per-program license fees are yours?

The allocation of income is done scientifically by survey. The various performing rights societies use different methods of allocation, and each swears its system is superior. In the case of radio airplay, stations are monitored. ASCAP currently receives radio airplay data from Media Monitors and RCS MediaBase as well as directly from radio stations not monitored by Media Monitors and RCS MediaBase. BMI uses RCS MediaBase, and SESAC uses BDS. What all of these systems do is take a scientifically selected group of radio stations and figure out what they are playing. If 20% of the radio stations are playing country music, then 20% of their radio station sampling will be of country stations. If 35% of the stations are hip-hop/rap stations, then 35% of their monitoring will be of hip-hop/rap stations.

These systems then figure out what this scientifically selected group of stations is playing. The Nielsen system that ASCAP uses, for example, monitors stations right off the air and a computer instantly matches the previously stored electronic "fingerprint" of a song (down to the artist and even particular mix) with what is being played. ASCAP also gets information directly from non-monitored radio stations, and satellite radio performance information from

SiriusXM. For each time the station picks up your song, you get an appropriate share of the performing right society's blanket and per-program license fee pool. If your big hit song comprises .00125% of the airplay in the country during a given quarter, then you will get .00125% of the royalty pool.

WHAT'S ON TV?

TV stations (and movie theaters overseas) also pay significant amounts into the license fee pools. This money is allocated according to what are known as cue sheets. A film or TV producer creates a cue sheet for a program that lists the name of the production (film name, or TV program name with episode name and number) and then all the music appearing in that program. The cue sheet lists the title of each music cue with the author, the publisher, type of use (theme, background vocal, background instrumental, visual performance, etc.), and the duration of usage. When the film or program is shown on TV, the performing right society electronically matches the applicable cue sheet with the airing and then knows who to credit and pay for the broadcast performance. (Again, in many foreign territories, based on cue sheet information, a pool of income is allocated to music publishers and songwriters out of theatrical box office receipts.)

Because the cue sheet is the basis for royalty payments, it is *very* important for songwriters and publishers to receive a copy of a cue sheet containing music they own or created. The songwriter/publisher should review the cue sheet for accuracy and then, although it may be a redundant submission (the producer should have submitted the cue sheet to ASCAP, BMI, and SESAC), submit it to his own performing right society and subpublishers (refer to the chapter on subpublishers) to ensure that anyone who might be in a position to pay him is able to do so.

The performing right societies work on a complete census of all the programs that are broadcast by television networks in the United States. If your music appears in a program that is broadcast on a network, and if a cue sheet that properly reflects your information has been sent to your performing right society, you should definitely receive a payment for the performance. The performing right societies are treating more and more stations in this manner all the time, including many cable channels.

If, however, the program in question airs on "spot" or syndicated TV, it is more difficult for the performing right societies to track usage in this way. Performance royalties from syndicated TV thus tend to be allocated based on a sampling (like radio) rather than a complete schedule-based census.

DO THEY MONITOR MY GYM?

We now understand radio and TV (hopefully). What about music being played in restaurants, stores, airplanes, aerobic studios, funeral homes, skating rinks, sports stadiums, and kids' gyms? Do the performing right societies monitor these places to see what is being played and to figure out what you're due? No way. Relatively speaking, the fees paid by these users are small. The performing right societies call musical performances in these venues nonsurveyed. That means no one is going to check what is being played there. The blanket license (and per-program) fees derived from these music users are nonetheless thrown into the distribution pool. The money gets allocated on the same basis as radio, TV, and other surveyed media in the same proportionate basis as those media. If you are getting .00125% of the total radio (and other surveyed) airplay during a given quarter, then they also throw in .00125% of the pool income relevant to nonsurveyed users.

It may surprise some people to know that an attempt is made to allocate by survey the performance fees paid by concert venues and arenas. Typically, a performing right society obtains a set list (list of songs played, including publishers and writers) either with respect to certain venues spread throughout the country (e.g., Staples Center in Los Angeles, Madison Square Garden in New York) or perhaps by selecting the ten biggest tours in a given year (Ed Sheeran, Taylor Swift, Left Alone). In this way, the societies introduce at least some survey data into the allocation of the performing right fees paid by these venues and tours.

THE ENFORCER

Every so often you will read in the paper about some poor schlub who is getting sued by ASCAP or another PRO. He thought that because he already bought the CD, the music was free to play in his restaurant or boutique or even on the telephone as hold music! Subject to certain size restrictions that exempt small businesses and restaurants, this is a mistaken belief.

When you buy a CD, you can listen to it in your car or home or wherever, but only for your personal use. For our purposes, "personal" also includes your family and friends when you play it at home or in the car. But if you want to perform the music contained on the CD in public for profit or other benefit at a business or restaurant exceeding the statutory exemption, that is a different animal, and you need a public performance license.

When ASCAP showed up at the schlub's restaurant and told him he needed a license if he was going to play ASCAP repertoire to create ambiance and help sell food and keep his restaurant trendy and popular and full, he told them where to go. He figured that it was just another shakedown like his payments to "Tony the protection guy" or the health inspector. He was wrong, and now ASCAP has sued him. He will lose the suit, and some lawyer will charge him to mount a hopeless defense. (But then again, he might also get a fair amount of ink in the local Thursday throwaway that he advertises in, so he can feel good about something.)

The amounts charged to these sundry venues by the performing right societies are relatively small, often a nominal amount that barely covers the cost of licensing. But the fees keep everything on the up-and-up while maintaining the legal principle that public performance of other people's music has to be paid for. When a performing right society calls a publisher and asks for a copy of the copyright certificate for "Light My Fire," someone is getting sued for nonlicensed public performance and is about to lose, in that order.

MY PERFORMING RIGHT SOCIETY
IS BETTER THAN YOURS

The performing right societies love to argue among themselves as to whose distribution system is best, and they all want to convince you that their system will result in your getting paid more if you please affiliate with them. One of the most ridiculous arguments is that "our survey of stations is twice as big as theirs." If the surveys are large enough to reduce the margin of error to an acceptable level, and if the science and statistics are good, it doesn't matter which survey is bigger. Look at it this way: let's say a survey of voters shows that 2 million voters, scientifically selected and surveyed out of 5 million total voters, favor a given candidate. If you double the survey size and find that 4 million voters out of 10 million total favor that candidate, you have learned nothing new. At a certain point in time, increasing your sample size does not tell you any new information. It only costs you more money. Likewise, if performing right society A pays you 10¢ every time your song gets picked up in its survey, but society B, which has twice as big a survey, only pays you 5¢ each time your song gets picked up in its survey, you will end up getting the same amount in the end because society B will pick you up twice as often but at half the rate. So don't worry about survey size or methodology too much.

Historically, BMI tended to pay its winners (songwriters and publishers with big hits) more money at the expense of the losers. Specifically, BMI has different bonus plateaus for rewarding songs that attained a lot of airplay. The plateaus were relative (e.g., your song is in the top 10% of airplay for BMI songs this quarter) rather than absolute (you got more than 100,000 airplays), so it was very hard to figure out where you stood. There was a basic rate they paid. Then there were "entry-level bonuses" (1.5 times the normal rate), "mid-level bonuses" (2.5 times the normal rate), and "super-level bonuses" (4 times the normal rate). So if you had a "small" song that got limited airplay, BMI would by necessity be paying you less so that it could pay the guy with the monstrous hit four times what he would ordinarily get.

Effective July 1, 2004, BMI instituted a new system to replace the four-tier bonus model. There are now three royalty payment components: a "current activity" payment, a "hit song bonus," and a "standards bonus." The current activity amount is based upon the actual fees paid by the station that played the song, rather than on a pool of blanket fees. The hit song bonus is for any work that has

95,000 performances in a given quarter. The amount to be allocated for hit song bonuses by BMI is not specified, and may or may not be fixed. The standards bonus is available to works with more than 2.5 million cumulative performances, and at least 15,000 performances in a given quarter. The standards bonus is also cumulative, which means that works with a high combination of current quarter and historical performances earn larger bonuses.

Compared to BMI, ASCAP tends to be more egalitarian: a radio airplay is worth what a radio airplay is worth. But ASCAP has instituted a single top-tier bonus (Radio Feature Premium) as well so that it pays out roughly the same amount of money to an ASCAP hit song as BMI would have otherwise paid out to that same hit song (isn't competition a wonderful thing?).

Competition in the United States between the performing right societies is often intense. From time to time, these organizations try to lure songwriters and publishers from each other and sometimes pay advances (or give "loans" or earnings guarantees) for a defection if the artist is important enough and makes a significant difference in the blanket and per-program licenses they can obtain from music users. My own opinion is that in most instances, a writer or publisher should go for the best performing right society and not be seduced by advances, which are basically transitory and not a function of quality.

How does one choose the "best" performing right society? Sometimes this choice is based on who provides you with the most support, encouragement, and assistance, but in most instances it comes down to who will pay you more for your performances. An interesting exercise is to compare payouts on split copyrights. Let's say you have a song that was written 50% by an ASCAP writer and 50% by a SESAC writer. (And of course we remember that we therefore have a 50% ASCAP publisher and a 50% SESAC publisher collecting the publishers' shares.) The song is a big hit and each writer (and publisher) receives his performing right statement from his respective performing right society. Oh, look at this! The ASCAP writer/publisher amount was $50,000 for the quarter, but the SESAC writer got $61,000. Does this really happen? Absolutely.

In my personal experience making such comparisons over many years, ASCAP has outpaid BMI except for a few cases involving big country hits when BMI trounced ASCAP. I can't draw a similar comparison with SESAC because I have only administered a few SESAC companies, and no split copyrights were involved. Many people in the industry have had different experiences, though. Putting aside the question of who pays the most, each of the PROs have their fans, with some people claiming that one society is more accommodating than another, or is more likely to respond quickly to a problem or issue. Difficult choices and trade-offs are involved in your choice of performing right society.

Lastly, know that in payment formulas, various weighting factors are applied to payouts, such as types of uses (a TV theme is worth more than a background "car radio playing" type use) and time of broadcast (prime time is better than 3:30 a.m. on Sunday morning), size of market, and other significant factors.

SYNCHRONIZATIONS

Unlike mechanical licensing, where there is a statutory rate or customary percentage basis to start from, and unlike performance licensing, where the licenses and rates are almost always handled by a third-party performing right society, synchronization licensing frequently requires a great deal of knowledge, decision making, and negotiating skill from the music publisher. Synchronization licensing and uses are thus among the most interesting and challenging areas in the publishing field.

The most important types of synchronization licenses involve television and motion picture productions. (Advertising often involves synchronizations but will be treated separately in the "Sundry Uses" chapter.) Many types of licenses are used in film and TV production, and the rule of thumb is the more they want, the more they pay. Myriad factors may be introduced into a negotiation, resulting in much different pricing and rates.

FILM FACTORS

Some of the factors a music publisher might consider as part of the decision and quoting process for a motion picture are listed below. It is extremely good business practice to require a potential film licensee to send a written request with as many of these variables spelled out as possible.

- The name of the picture, the stars, the director, the distributors, studio and/or financiers, the projected film rating, the budget, and a plot synopsis.

- How the film proposes to use your song, including the type of use (background instrumental, background vocal, opening credits, closing credits, repeated theme, etc.) and the duration(s).

- A specific scene description and a few pages of script indicating the proposed use in context.

- The type and duration of rights that you are to be quoting on. Is it for a fixed period of years (five? ten?) or for perpetuity? (As an aside, it is inadvisable to quote for perpetuity since the rights you have under copyright law are not for perpetuity but for a fixed period of years. If you grant rights that you don't have, you could get in trouble. Whenever you see the word *perpetuity,* try to remember to cross it out and replace it with "life of copyright, plus renewals and extensions.") In which media do they want to include the song (movie theaters, television, on-demand streaming services, home video devices, "technology now known or hereinafter devised," etc.)?

- The territory for which the rights are desired (United States, the World, and now, frequently, the Universe).

- Which master recording of your song they will be using (if there is more than one), or if they plan to rerecord the song themselves. Remember, too, that the film production will need to license your musical composition (PA copyright) and license (or create) a master (SR copyright) recording.

- Whether they want the song for ancillary uses ("making of" documentaries or other featurettes, trailers, advertising, sequels, soundtrack albums, etc.).

Of course, before formulating a quote, you should always ask yourself the question: "Is this a film I want this song to be in?" You might not even have to consider any of the foregoing!

Most major studios and film productions will now simply ask you to quote on a *broad rights license.* What they mean by this is usually a worldwide license for a duration of the life of copyright, plus renewals and extensions, covering usage within the *linear film* (as opposed to excerpted outside of the use within the film) in theaters, television, home video devices, on-demand streaming, future linear motion picture devices or transmission methods, and in-context advertising, in-context promotions, and in-context trailers. But if they just tell you that they want *broad rights*, it is advisable to have them spell out what they consider *broad rights* to actually be, as you want to be quoting on the same thing they think they are buying.

An aside about *in-context* is in order here. *In-context* refers to uses of a song as it appears within a film. The scene and exact visual images in the same timed relationship that they appear within the motion picture represent an in-context use. If a film uses your song where a man is seen chopping down a tree, an in-context use will always have that same man chopping down that same tree to your song. *Out of context* would be where a production lifts your song as separate music from that scene and then uses it, for example, as a musical bed for a television commercial or theatrical trailer where many other scenes and images are used.

It is common, but by no means an absolute requirement, to grant in-context uses within a broad rights motion picture license. In this way, the studio is free to have its stars go on talk shows and show clips of scenes that include your music, and not have to strip out your background music. The same applies to in-context use within trailers, advertising, and other promotions for the motion picture. The music publisher is cautioned, though, to be possibly redundant by adding the words *in-context* in a quote for a license request that asks for "additional use in in-context trailers, advertising, clips, and promotions." Since it is not definitively clear whether the requestor's use of *in-context* is intended to modify just *trailers* or also *advertising, clips,* and *promotions,* it is wise to indicate on the request that you are quoting on "in-context trailers, in-context advertising, in-context clips, and in-context promotions." Once you've had an argument with a film studio as to what *in-context* was supposed to modify, you will never forget to make this clarification again.

Broad rights licenses are almost always granted on a flat-fee basis. They pay you once, and that is it. There will be no additional fees for TV broadcast, streaming on-demand, airplane showings, or home video devices like Blu-ray discs and DVDs. Also, the fee paid to a record company to license a given master recording of a publisher's song is usually (but not absolutely) on a most favored nations basis with that master. It is rare that a master recording quote is allowed to be higher than a music publisher's corresponding quote. Here's a hypothetical situation in which that might occur: let's say someone is making a film about the group The Doors and thinking of including only one of their "outside" cover recordings, such as Berthold Brecht's and Kurt Weill's "Whiskey Bar" or Willie Dixon's "Back Door Man." In this instance, the producer might decide that the most important thing relevant to the movie is Jim Morrison singing the song and The Doors playing the music (it's Doors-ness) and not the underlying composition. The producer might want to include only one "outside" song and simply choose "Whiskey Bar" or "Back Door Man" depending on which publisher quotes the lesser amount, while paying The Doors' record company a higher fee for the master. (It can also work the other way. Maybe they just *need* to have "Light My Fire," and then they pay some starving musician a pittance to make and license them a cheap master recording.)

Fees for broad rights synchronization licenses vary widely. An unknown or little-known song within the body of a major studio motion picture may get anywhere (as a typical range) from $10,000 to $20,000, on a MFN basis with the master recording. Those fees might double if the song is used over credits. A known but non-hit song might fetch from $20,000 to $30,000. A hit song, a song recorded or written by a major artist, or a standard-type song might obtain from $30,000 to $100,000 or more. An iconic song ("Satisfaction," "Yesterday," or "Whole Lotta Love," for example) might command several hundred thousand dollars. These quotes, too, are subject within reason to the size of the film's budget and the fame of its stars and director. A $400 million Spielberg *E.T.* sequel would certainly justify a higher quote than a $500,000 production of *Porky's 12: The Fifth Day After the First Week*.

In my experience, a significant synchronization license of a song not specifically written for a given production is always *nonexclusive*. Music publishers want to retain the right to license their songs to other films and TV productions. An *exclusive* license could be issued, but it would have a hugely deleterious impact on the value of a song if it could never be licensed again.

Sometimes, a film production doesn't want (or can't afford) broad rights and a music publisher is asked to quote on limited rights, or sometimes limited rights with priced options for expanded future uses. Some sample limitations might be a request to quote on: "broad rights for the United States only, with an option to be exercised within two years for use in the film outside of the United States"; "limited theatrical (50 screens or less) and television media only"; or even a hybrid by territory such as "television and home video for the United States, but television, home video, and theatrical outside of the United States." The expected corollary to the more they want, the more they pay, is the less they want, the less they pay. Lower budget productions often try to carve out the acquisition of rights they don't really need, to try and obtain a reduced quote for their immediate needs.

HALF THE WORLD

A few rules of thumb for quoting on less than broad rights can be useful. The United States is typically treated as "half the world" from a music business standpoint. The rest of the world, often referred to as ROW, gets the other half. So a U.S. broad rights license would be priced at about half of what a worldwide broad rights license would cost. If you were granting an option for ROW broad rights, you would want to have a limited time period during which the producer had the right to exercise it (two years?), and you would want the total split fee of both the United States and ROW broad rights licenses to be greater than if they paid for the World (or Universe) all at once. (You should get more than the total lump sum cost if they are paying you in two portions, especially if the second payment isn't guaranteed. A 20% uplift on each half of the whole worldwide fee might be appropriate.)

It is important for a publisher to maintain a respectable minimum value to a copyright. If you license the Doors' "Light My Fire" to one low-budget picture for $10,000, and then try to license it later to a high-budget picture for $400,000, you might find the negotiations are difficult if the studio has somehow found out that you took $10,000 last month from the earlier production. The value of music and the importance of maintaining a copyright's long-term viability is discussed elsewhere in this book.

OUT-OF-CONTEXT USES

Frequently, once a song's use has been confirmed in a film, a production or marketing department may then want to acquire additional ancillary or out-of-context uses. An ancillary use example might be wanting to use a song as a DVD menu musical background (which is also an out-of-context use). The most common request is for out-of-context trailers and/or TV advertising. This is advertising for the film that may be shown in motion picture theater trailers, or on television, which uses your song as a non-contextural musical bed. The trailer might make use of your song throughout all or a substantial portion of its duration, even though your song may have only appeared within the film for ten seconds or even not at all. It is also very common for film studios to want to use music to advertise a film that doesn't even appear within the film.

The production budget is usually responsible for the payment of synchronization fees for songs appearing in the film. Sometimes film synchronization fees are even paid for or partially underwritten by a record company that will be putting out a corresponding soundtrack album. However, the marketing budget may be paid for out of a different budget entirely, and even if the film production is over budget and flat broke, the marketing budget might be flush with pre-allocated money ready to be spent. Sometimes, for example, in the case of a so-called *negative pickup* where a studio obtains distribution to an independently produced film, the party paying for marketing and advertising isn't the same party that produced the film.

It is not unreasonable to quote the same amount for an out-of-context trailer fee as you got for the song being licensed in the motion picture itself. If they paid you $50,000 to synchronize your song in the film itself, then quoting an additional $50,000 for out-of-context trailers and advertising would also be reasonable. And again, on a most favored nations basis with the co-publisher and corresponding master recording, right?

For out-of-context trailer uses in the circumstance where a song doesn't even appear in the film itself, most music publishers elect to treat the situation as a straight advertisement using the song and charge more than if the song were in the film. In other words, the usage is not viewed as supplemental income. Fees for out-of-context usage in trailers and advertising when a song is not in the film it is promoting are often in the range of $40,000 to $100,000 and up, depending on how well the song is known by the public and how well it fits in with the film it would be used to advertise. (The life of a film and its eventual home video release, and the corresponding advertising and marketing windows, are usually very short.) And again, on a most favored nations basis with the co-publisher and corresponding master recording, as always, right?

I AIN'T GOT NO MONEY THAT I CAN DEPEND ON

The bane of your existence as a music publisher just might be the student or independent filmmaker. The good news at least is that the film schools are teaching new filmmakers that film music isn't free, and getting them grounded in the licensing process. The bad news is that 50 million (maybe 49 million?) of these people want music licenses and have no money to pay for them. Without exception, they always want the most valuable or special song of your most guarded songwriter, the guy who never approves anything anyway and who hardly ever answers your inquiries in less than two months. Typically, it costs you more money to issue a license to these filmmakers than you get from them, and it takes you more time than you have to spend. In short, the Law of Inverse Effort is in action.

A reasonable compromise, at least for film school students, is a limited *film festival license*. These are usually one or two-page documents, with a specified term typically from one to three years, limiting exhibition only to not-for-profit film festivals, classroom use, and maybe a small number of video copies for friends and family (say, 25 copies?). Fees are typically from $250 to $750. It is important, too, since you will generally not be wasting your time reading the script and screening the movie, that the license state clearly that it is being granted on a non-precedential basis (meaning that you won't be required to do it that way again), and that you are under no future expressed or implied obligation to license the work for any additional media, period of time, or other circumstance whatsoever. And once the young filmmaker starts having her spinster sister-in-law, the maritime law attorney, calling you to negotiate the deal, it's time to cut loose and run.

It is also advisable, for film festival licenses, to pre-negotiate the broad rights option fee, and to further specify that your song won't be taken out of the film once they get distribution. It's always a real bummer to do a favor for someone by giving them a cheap film festival license to help them sell the film and get distribution and then have them yank your song from the film once they have a real budget to spend on music for a full theatrical release.

Independent films and documentaries are tougher calls. You never know what film is going to be the next *Lost in Translation* or an independent box office megahit. On the one hand, it would be nice to have a song in a big well-known film; on the other hand, simply "nice" doesn't do it unless you're also getting paid. A step deal clause (as discussed in the chapter called "The Value of Music") might be considered. Typical wording for this sort of clause would be something like:

"If and when the Motion Picture attains gross receipts of $20 million dollars, Producer shall pay to Publisher within 30 days thereafter an additional fee of $10,000. If and when the Motion Picture attains gross receipts of $30 million dollars, Producer shall pay to Publisher within 30 days thereafter a further additional fee of $10,000. Said additional payments are payable based on actual gross receipts whether or not publicly reported, although Publisher and Producer both agree that figures reported in such trade publications as *Variety*, *Hollywood Reporter*, or advertisements relating to the Motion Picture in such publications shall be deemed accurate."

As for documentaries, producers will frequently push for a low synchronization fee on the basis that documentaries don't make much money and aren't widely exhibited or seen. This seems to be changing though. In 2018, one documentary ("Won't You Be My Neighbor?") made almost $25 million at the box office, and three others exceeded $10 million in receipts (L.A. Times, April 25, 2019).

THERE'S NEVER ANYTHING ON TV

Television music synchronization licenses are similar to film licenses in many ways except the fees are lower and the media requested is usually only TV (and maybe common carriers such as cruise ships and airlines) and frequently on-demand streaming services (which seem to be replacing the DVD/home video market). Many TV programs don't even make it past a few episodes or ever make it to the point where they are aired outside of the United States. It is very common to get TV synchronization license requests with limited terms and territories. These quote requests are often replete with options that the producer can exercise if and when the show runs past its third episode, gets sold overseas, ends up on home video or streaming services, etc. You have to be a genius sometimes to figure out how to quote on the myriad ways some producers want you to quote.

A typical request might be for a quote for two years, U.S. and Canada, for all television media. Again, many of the bullet points discussed above with respect to film licensing are applicable. A fee in the $2,500 to $6,500 range might be appropriate. A 24-month option might be requested for the right to obtain all television rights, worldwide, for the life of copyright and renewals. A supplemental fee (make sure it is very clear that this is in addition to the initial fee and not instead of it) in the $5,500 to $8,000 range might be appropriate. A fee for unlimited streaming and the manufacture of home video devices (referred to as a *video buyout*) is typically in the $8,000 to $12,000 range.

For established TV shows that have passed the point in their existence of sweating whether they will be picked up for another season, the producers often obtain worldwide television and streaming/home video rights quotes. *The Simpsons* is a good example of the type of show that would need long-term television rights and also streaming/home video rights. When everything is licensed, paid for, and quoted up front, a typical use for all television, worldwide, for the life of copyrights and renewals might go for $8,000 to $12,000. Streaming and home video rights in the form of a buyout would also be in the $8,000 to $12,000 range, and you might give the producers a little break if they pay for the TV rights and the streaming/video buyout not as an option but at the same time. Iconic songs may get even more, and new or "breaking" songs might get less. And what is our mantra? Most favored nations with the co-publisher and master recording. You may even wish to extend your most favored nations requirement to include all songs and master recordings in the program or episode if your song has that clout.

VIDEO LICENSES

There are many types of home video programs. Most motion picture licenses already include streaming/home video rights as part of the initial flat fee. Likewise, many, but not all, TV synchronization licenses make provisions for a home video (DVD, Blu Ray, streaming, etc.) flat-fee buyout. The types of programs that aren't covered in this way are discussed here.

Such programs would typically consist of material that has a more limited audience. Examples might be for a Discovery or National Geographic channel program on fruit bats that will be released on DVD for all of 5,000 people to buy and available on Netflix to fruit bat enthusiasts and anyone else on-demand. A video producer might then offer a lower than usual streaming/video buyout due to the smaller audience, perhaps with some sort of unit cap and time limit, for instance, $2,500 for up to 25,000 units distributed or streamed for up to seven years. An alternative might be a royalty-based approach with a per-unit fee of anywhere from 10¢ to 14¢, maybe with a smaller ($500 to $1,000?) advance. This approach, analogous to a video mechanical license, is also used frequently in home video programs where the music is more significant, such as concert video DVDs. (Because the audio-only statutory rate is 9.1¢, a publisher really wouldn't want to quote less than that penny rate given that an audiovisual use is an enhanced "better" use and should cost more.)

THE CHANGING WORLD

As with CD sales, the home video paradigm is rapidly changing from an ownership model to models that involve subscriptions, pay-per-view, streaming and video on-demand (VOD), electronic sell-through, and ad-supported streaming. I've had a lot of people complain that DVDs and Blu Ray discs aren't selling any more, and they should pay less for their home video music rights. But all those lost physical sales are going to other forms of delivery, so as you lower your physical home video quotes, you should be raising your alternative electronic delivery fees to match. Really, the same holds true, too, with television. Fewer and fewer people are now watching programs live in real time. Rather, they are recording the shows, or more likely streaming them off of programing websites at times and places that are more convenient for them. Millions of people are watching things via Amazon.com, the Google Play Store, network websites, MLB.TV, Hulu, and Netflix. So if you're quoting less for TV as the medium currently exists, and if the viewership is staying somewhat constant, you should be correspondingly raising the quote for other forms of programing delivery. The internet is the new TV.

IT WAS HERE A SECOND AGO

Some types of visual synchronized uses are termed ephemeral. The Copyright Act provides for what are called *ephemeral uses* without the permission of the copyright owner. Ephemeral uses are generally "live" or "live tape delay" type uses where the exploitation is made spontaneously and the necessity of obtaining advance permission would place an undue or impossible burden on the music user.

The only income the writer and publisher receive for an ephemeral use is performance income collected by ASCAP, BMI, or other performing right society.

Some recognized examples of ephemeral uses are the incidental background broadcast use at a baseball or football game, live news program uses, and parade broadcasts. *Saturday Night Live, The Tonight Show,* and *The Late Show* may also be considered ephemeral uses for which no advance permission is legally required. (Note, however, once the original programs are rebroadcast—such as on *The Best of Saturday Night Live* or *The Best of The Late Show,* or when they go on vacation and have to show re-runs for a few weeks—they are no longer ephemeral uses and the appropriate party must obtain a synchronization license!)

There are also gray cases that producers claim are ephemeral, but these may not meet certain legal criteria. Many soap operas and broadcast news magazines such as *60 Minutes*, for instance, try to squeak by as ephemeral users. A music publisher sufficiently concerned with this matter might wish to retain a copyright attorney to handle and examine the legal issues more thoroughly.

THAT'S BS! NO, IT'S PBS

Songwriters and publishers sometimes get upset when they see their works synchronized on PBS shows without permission. Guess what? They don't need your permission. Congress has granted PBS the equivalent of a compulsory synchronization license (refer to the chapter on mechanical licensing if you don't remember what compulsory licensing is). PBS may use any of your works that have been publicly distributed without your permission as long as they comply with the copyright laws on compulsory synchronization licensing. The government wanted to help public, not-for-profit broadcasters and gave them this gift. PBS pays a very small fee for each such use according to a schedule determined by law. Once a year, after your song has been used by PBS, they track you down, ask you to confirm your ownership, and then send you a check. The amount isn't very big, but you've helped support public broadcasting in your own little way, like it or not.

Note, though, that they *only have PBS broadcast rights* on this compulsory basis. If PBS wants to sell home videos (or give away DVDs as viewer donation premiums), or if they want to sell or distribute their programming to another outlet such as the Discovery Channel or Netflix, this is not covered and they need a license. Unless you are inclined to treat such extra-PBS exploitation as a donation of sorts, they should be paying fair market value for their income-generating exploitations.

THOSE FOREIGNERS DID WHAT?

The usual convention is that synchronization licenses are issued in the territory where the production is based even if the license is to cover the entire world. United States music publishers typically employ various parties (or have foreign divisions) to represent their repertoire throughout the world. These foreign representatives are called subpublishers. It is customary for the original publisher to grant various subpublishers the right, subject to the original publisher's approval, to grant worldwide synchronization license for works produced within the subpublisher's territory.

Thus, a film produced in England that requires a worldwide synchronization license typically contacts the applicable English subpublisher. Likewise, worldwide synchronization licenses for productions based in Japan look to Japanese subpublishers, and so forth. Almost all films and TV shows shown in the United States are made in the English language and are thus the primary concern of most United States music publishers. Unfortunately, foreign subpublishers often take a more laissez-faire approach to synchronization licenses for films and TV shows that are in foreign languages and are unlikely ever to be seen in the United States.

Throughout the world outside of the United States, English-language films and TV programs are produced primarily in the U.K., Canada, Australia, and New Zealand. Unlike in the United States, where $100 million to $200 million budgets are common, most foreign English-language films and programs are made with more modest budgets. Consequently, synchronization fees for English-language films produced outside of the United States also tend to be more modest. Nonetheless, if a foreign English-language film has significant stars and directors and will be opening "wide" (i.e., 1,000 to 3,000 screens or more) in the United States, there is no reason why the synchronization fee charged by the applicable subpublisher to the foreign English-language film production shouldn't be the same as if the film were a domestic production.

Foreign-language films wishing to use a publisher's music usually get a much better price because the exposure and distribution that their film (or TV program) will receive is far more limited. The best advice as to what a synchronization license should cost in a foreign territory is often received from the original publisher's local agent, the subpublisher.

In the mechanical licensing chapter, we talked about how in some ways, local mechanical right societies are detrimentally affecting their principals' rights by competing over central licensing agreements. Another way that some foreign mechanical and/or performing right societies are hurting their principals and eroding the value of their property is by offering film and/or TV producers blanket licenses covering synchronizations.

In the United States, music publishers ordinarily have the right to say, "No, I don't want my song to be in that TV show, and I won't issue a synchronization license." However, due to the existence of foreign blanket synchronization license arrangements, some TV and film producers in some territories automatically include the publisher's work in a program without the need for any formal permission. All the producers have to do is pay the specified fee or tariff to the local rights society where the original publisher's works have been registered.

For example, neither the BBC or Channel 4 in England require any formal approval to synchronize your music if your works are part of the local mechanical right society (MCPS) repertoire. They just have to pay the specified fee. Besides unconscionably denying the publisher the right to review and decline or approve a proposed use, such rates tend to be far less than would be negotiated in an arm's length agreement. In fact, the specified rates tend to be given as rate per second, such as £8/second. The characteristics of neither the particular song nor the production are considered. Additionally, such blanket-granted synchronization licenses tend to be overly broad, and also often include home video devices.

Why would a foreign rights society do this? Simply because it is an easy, automatic way to collect (and commission) greater income. It would be much better in these situations if the original publisher's local subpublisher, not the local rights society, controlled synchronization licensing. The local subpublisher has the original publisher's interests at heart; the subpublisher wants to make money and keep the original publisher's account by keeping him happy, and has similar interests in the long-term value of a copyright.

I am aware of some publishers in England who are now not registering works with the local mechanical right society, MCPS, for this very reason. Instead, these publishers are directly collecting mechanical income from the applicable record label (as we do here in the United States) and not through a mechanical rights society. By not registering these works with MCPS, the publishers are not subjecting their works to blanket synchronization licenses and the often embarrassingly low fees charged for them. Instead, these publishers are retaining approval over the uses of their works in audiovisual media.

In response to pressure from such publishers, and as now required by European trade directive, collective rights managers (CRMs) such as MCPS (which nonetheless denies it is a CRM) are starting to allow publishers to withdraw various categories of uses such as blanket synchronization licenses. In the new deal between MCPS and the BBC, publishers are given the freedom to opt out of blanket synchronization licensing. This is a huge and important paradigm shift.

LEAST FAVORED NATIONS

Another aside about most favored nations quotes is in order here. A few of the studios have decreed that it is now their policy not to license songs on a most favored nations basis, or to grant limited most favored nations protection only with respect to the co-publisher and/or corresponding master recording. Just remember, though, that these "written in stone" corporate policies are arbitrary, unilaterally determined, and not to your benefit. You may well have your own corporate policy that says you only issue licenses on Thursdays, or that you won't deal with people who have the letter e in their first name, or even that you only grant licenses that include most favored nations protection. You are the only one who owns and can license this particular song (unless you have a co-publisher on a split copyright). Your song is unique in the world, and why should their corporate policy trump your corporate policy? Just because they're bigger than you?

If you have a genuine concern that the studio may be paying more for other similar songs and uses in the same program, or if you simply want to make sure that they are not, you may *not* want to give on this point. But, being branded as difficult or unreasonable (meaning, you won't do exactly what they want you to do) can result in a publisher having fewer or no new requests from a given TV or film studio, so be careful. These (and other similar) battles should be fought only when the stakes are significant and when the principle truly matters to you, a songwriter, or client. Arriving at a mutually satisfactory compromise is preferable.

The only time I feel strongly about going to the wall on a most favored nations dispute is when an original quote and/or confirmation letter was made on that basis. Trying to remove most favored nations wording once the formal licensing process gets underway is an underhanded and dishonest thing to do. (It's the licensing equivalent of, "Oh, you wanted floor mats with the car?") If your accepted quote included MFN wording, then some corporate lawyer citing "corporate policy written in stone" has no legal, moral, or ethical right to deprive you of a very valuable (but nonfinancial) component of the deal once licensing has begun. This kind of maneuver also means, in many cases, that someone else is getting a better deal than you and they don't want you to know it.

Sometimes all it takes to make you feel like you're getting something in return for giving up the MFN benefit is to have a few thousand dollars more thrown in. This way, the studio can feel big and strong and know that its almighty arbitrary corporate policy has withstood yet another unworthy assault.

WHAT DOES IT ALL MEAN ANYWAY?

Much discussion has been given to the importance of most favored nations wording. It is an unfortunate truth that MFN is beginning to mean very little. Dishonest record companies and film producers have found so many duplicitous ways to make you think that no one is receiving more money than you are for a given use, that you have to wonder whether anyone is dealing fairly and honestly, with any modicum of good faith. Where there's a dishonest will, there's a dishonest way, and virtually anyone can find a loophole in an MFN clause big enough to drive a truck through.

Here are some real world things that can and do happen:

- You are offered "MFN with similar songs and uses." So what is to stop them from paying someone else double the fee you are getting because their use is actually an "interrupted" use that they are treating as a second use and paying a second fee?

- You are offered "MFN with similar songs and rights granted." Sounds innocent enough until they clear your song for life of copyright, and the other guy's song for "perpetuity," and pay him three times as much because the rights granted are dissimilar. Or maybe you both cleared the rights for life of copyright, but the other guy also included Internet streaming in his quote, and you didn't.

- You are offered "MFN with all songs used." But meanwhile, they are paying a supplemental "talent fee," "consultation fee," or "travel expense" to the other guy. I know this happens because I've seen my clients receive such perks above and beyond the MFN fee. One of my clients got a $50,000 fee for a two-page written analysis of a particular car stereo in addition to the 2¢ MFN per unit he received for being on the demonstration disc that came with each new car. Sometimes they even clear and pay for songs they don't use ("The scene was cut out at the last minute but we had already paid the fee") just to get around the MFN restrictions and pay someone else more. Or the producers offer to make a donation to the charity of your choice if you agree to the MFN rate.

- You demand, receive, and are proud of yourself for getting a "100,000 unit advance, MFN, in exchange for granting a 75% of statutory mechanical rate" for the compilation album *Songs That Start with the Letter S*. But the record company people, meanwhile, are interpreting the MFN to mean that they are not paying anyone who is granting a 75% rate an advance of more than 100,000 units. But meanwhile, three other publishers with songs on the same album are getting *no advance* but full statutory royalties. (I try to get around this one by asking for "MFN with respect to both advance *and* rate paid.")

It really comes down to the fact that offering MFN terms is a way to induce you to go along with the pack mentality, and to do what "everyone else is doing." But sometimes the licenser simply can't get everyone to go along with his offered rate, and is faced with huge costs of paying everyone a higher rate. ("I've got 300 songs in the mini-series, and I can't pay everyone $2,000 more per song just because you think my offer is too low. How about if I fly you and your client to meet with the director in Florence, first class, for eight nights?") That's when the bending of truth, fairness, and agreements begins.

COMING BACK FOR MORE

In the last few years, many new technologies and entertainment delivery systems have been developed and are coming into common use. It wasn't so long ago that home video (initially VHS and Beta videotapes) didn't exist. Then there were DVDs, Blu-ray, podcasts, iTunes videos, VOD (video on-demand), Internet streaming, TiVo, SanDisc slot players, 3D TV, 4K versions, etc., etc. Who knows what tomorrow will bring?

Many media companies, especially film and TV program owners, hadn't adequately anticipated the future and find themselves lacking rights for new technologies that they wished they had. I remember a major studio coming to me for a music-intensive teen movie that came out in the 1970s for which it had acquired the rights to sell up to 50,000 home video devices. At the time, that threshold must have seemed like a lot for the new technology, but once the studio cleared additional rights for a huge chunk of change, the movie went on to sell millions of copies.

The studios are now being a bit more savvy and are typically asking for all rights "now known or hereinafter devised," sometimes also referred to as "future technologies." The sad part is that they want to pay the same fees for, as an example, TV, streaming, home video, and future technologies as they used to pay just for TV and home video rights. It ought to be that if you're giving them more rights, you receive more money, but "future technologies" seem so vague and intangible to most people (except the studios that have now learned better!) that they are often thrown into the same bundle for no extra compensation.

It still happens quite a bit, though, that music licensers will come back to clear rights that they missed the first time around. Most likely they got home video rights if the film or program was made in the last 30 years, but in looking to the future, they want to close any loopholes while they are still intangible and (they hope) reasonably priced. So it is common to hear from someone inquiring about something you licensed 20 years ago saying, "How much would it cost us to 'upgrade' our rights to include future technologies?" (Sometimes this is called "perfecting" the rights.) In recent years, I've been approached about clearing additional rights for *Saturday Night Live* DVD box sets, *The Dick Cavett Show, Miami Vice,* and even *Freaks and Geeks* for which the initial rights acquired were not sufficient for modern exploitation.

In many ways this is a windfall for the publisher at the expense of users who didn't buy all the rights they eventually realized they wanted the first time around. If you got a good fee for the initial rights, the typical going fee right now for upgrading existing licenses to include "now known or hereinafter devised" future technologies might be 25% of the original fee. For example, if you got $20,000 for TV and home video the first time around, you might charge an additional $5,000 today for the upgrade to anything they can think of in the future. However, if you got a low or inappropriate fee the first time around, you can make a good case to quote much more for the future technology upgrade at this time.

A FEW MORE DO'S AND DON'TS

A publisher should not give an indefinite open-ended quote for any type of synchronization license. A given quote should always have an expiration date. Legally speaking, options are recognized as having an economic value. If you are giving someone an option to use your song ten years from now, you should be compensated for that option. Giving quotes with a 60 or 90-day period of acceptance is a good way to protect a copyright. If the decision has not been made on whether or not to use a song, or if the production or postproduction has not been completed, a publisher can always agree to re-quote a proposed use or agree to extend the term for which the prior quote is still valid.

When giving a quote (and all requests and quotes should always be in writing), it is a good idea to indicate that a given quote is "subject to a signed written license, and payment of the specified fees." Don't blur the line and have the written quote serve as an integrated (complete) license form in and of itself. The reason is because a good license form will have many terms other than the basic licensed media, uses, terms, and fees that will be beneficial to both parties. These may include the specification of legal venue (California, New York, English Law, etc.); restrictions on editing or arranging a song to fit the picture; and requirements that the producer prepare and submit an accurate cue sheet to the publisher and applicable performing right societies (so the publisher can receive performance income), provide for mutual indemnifications, and provide for screen credits of the writer and/or publisher; and many other very important terms.

In the case of a song owned partially (say, 50%) by a publishing company, it is also advisable for a given quote to be not only on a most favored nations basis with the corresponding master recording but with the co-publisher, while watching for the pitfalls described above. You don't want the production to pay you less for the license of your half of the song than he is getting for the license of the other half of the song. Likewise, if the song is split unequally, you want the most favored nations to apply on a prorated basis. For this reason, many music publishers give a quote with the notation that "quote is based on 100% of copyright, prorated for our share" to indicate both most favored nations (with the co-publisher) intent and to remind the licenser that they don't possess all the ownership in a given song.

On a co-published song, you might also be told that your co-publisher has already agreed to a fee. And hypothetically speaking, they may have told your co-publisher that you already agreed to a fee. Check with your co-publisher directly before you go along with the quote. You may well hear something like "I told them I'd be OK with the fee if it was OK with you," which is a lot different than "He already agreed to this fee." This really happens. A lot.

Watch out, too, for requests for quotes on overly broad rights and seeming boilerplate wording. For example, a lot of MTV and VH1 quote requests now want you to quote on use "in the Program, in whole or in part." What does "in part" mean? It means that even though you quoted on your song being used on the *MTV Video Music Awards 2019,* you might also be giving them the right to excerpt the artist's performance of your song in another program, say *Snoop Dogg: Home for Christmas,* when your intent was to license the song for use in one program only. Read and think about what you are quoting on, and don't be afraid to make changes or add restrictions. If *American Idol* states that payment will be made once the use is confirmed and the season finale has been broadcast, you might want to say, "Hey, wait a minute, why can't they pay me once they've made the use? Why do I have to wait until after the season finale if you used my song in the second episode of the season?"

Here's another one I started objecting to once I actually started thinking about seemingly innocuous language. TV producers will throw in "motion picture theaters where a separate admission fee is charged." So what does that mean? I'm just giving them permission for a few "free" screenings? Well how many times have you ever been charged a "separate admission fee" to a film festival or double feature for each work shown, or for movie that is preceded by a "short" or cartoon? You just pay one fee to get in, not a "separate" fee for each thing shown at the same festival. So basically if you agree to throw in theatrical subject to a "separate" admission fee, you may have just given them theatrical rights for nothing.

When I was first learning how to drive, my mother used to tell me that when driving I should always pretend that the rest of the world was crazy and unpredictable. Well, in licensing, maybe it's not a half bad idea to be a little paranoid, and assume that everyone else is out to screw you?

Finally, please remember, too, that fees given in this chapter are subjective opinions. Paradigms and norms change quickly, and until you develop an ongoing and dynamic feel for pricing, you should consult with others more knowledgeable of current industry norms.

CONFIRMATION LETTERS

Productions often send music publishers confirmation letters detailing the terms of a synchronization quote that has been given by the publisher. It is a good idea to carefully review these confirmation letters for accuracy, to make appropriate changes where necessary, and to indicate again that the quote given is "subject to a signed written license, and payment of the specified fees." The confirmation letters are often prepared by music clearing houses and not the producers themselves. The unfortunate reality is that many of these music clearance houses are very amateurish, unknowledgeable, dishonest, and sloppy. (But other than that, they're fine.) The confirmation letters they send you usually contain a statement to the effect that they are "proceeding in reliance" of your quote, and thus while they are trying to legally bind you to an offer to license, they are doing so before they themselves have confirmed that they will in fact be using your song. Legally speaking, they are trying to protect themselves against potential licensing problems through detrimental reliance. Within commonsense limits, it is reasonable for them to want to have you on the hook to agree to license a song to them (a binding quote) even though they aren't necessarily on the hook to use the song until the film is finished, edited, and ready for theatrical distribution. But this is specifically why you will again want to verify the terms in the confirmation letter and to have it be subject to a formal written signed license (to be negotiated in good faith) and the receipt of the payment of the sums you have quoted.

STREAMING, THE MUSIC MODERNIZATION ACT, AND THE CRB

The biggest game changer right now is how people consume music. In the past, music as a consumer product was bought as a physical unit. While some of today's music consumers still like owning a physical product such as a CD or a vinyl disk, or as a digital file, today's consumer is seeing great benefit in a streaming "access" model. In the streaming access model, the music resides as an electronic file on the remote servers of others, and can be listened to when desired. It is not a sale or download in the traditional sense, or anything that is owned by the consumer. One of the primary benefits is the ability to listen to virtually any piece of music at any time, which is great for consumers because they aren't restricted to listening to what they've already bought. It's a "why buy the cow when you can have milk anytime you want" model. And the streaming format has the further benefit of being able to handle audiovisual uses in addition to audio-only uses.

The companies offering streaming services have several different financial models. The streams may be free to the user and funded by ads or paid for by the user on a subscription basis. The streams may or may not also be available "on-demand." On-demand means that the user interacts with the service and determines what she wants to listen to or view, as compared to "lean-back" streaming services which determine which songs to stream for the user with minimal user interaction and control. Many of the popular streaming services offer a mix of ad-supported and paid tiers (e.g. Spotify Free vs. Spotify Premium and Pandora vs. Pandora Plus) and on-demand and lean-back options (e.g. Pandora vs. Pandora Premium and

Apple Music On-Demand Streaming vs. Apple Music Beats 1 Radio). Other types of access models might be in the form of "bundles" with mobile phone providers (you pay a monthly fee and you get your phone calls and your music). Most streaming companies also offer discounted family and student plans (which yield discounted royalty rates).

Streaming is a unique animal in that the Digital Performance Right in Sound Recordings Act of 1995 (and subsequently the courts) has determined that an on-demand stream consists of both a mechanical right component and a performing right component, whereas lean-back streaming only consists of a performance component not unlike traditional "terrestrial" radio broadcasts. Consequently, each on-demand stream of a song generates a performance royalty that the service pays to the appropriate performing rights organization such as ASCAP, BMI, SESAC or GMR (which is then subsequently paid to the writers and publishers), as well as a mechanical royalty that is paid directly to the publisher. Lean-back streams, however, only generate a performance royalty. Don't forget, too, that the streaming service also needs to license the use of the master (sound recording) from the record company (who then must account to the artist). (Lean-back performances also throw off a SoundExchange royalty on the master side.)

To summarize, streaming services license and pay:

On-Demand Streams
PUBLISHERS: mechanical and performance components;
                                and
LABELS: master recording license fees

Lean-Back Streams
PUBLISHERS: performance rights/royalties; and
LABELS: SoundExchange royalties

Obviously, the streaming services can only pay out so much *in total* if they want to stay in business, which sets the stage for a three-way tussle for parts of that total pool between record labels, publishers, and performance rights organizations. Unfortunately, the DSPs knew they could avail themselves of the compulsory license for mechanical rights, and get automatic consent decree licenses for the performing rights (at least with respect to ASCAP and BMI), whereas the labels were in a free market without mandatory licensing. The DSPs either made a calculated business decision or were somewhat naïve (or both), but in dealing with the publishers last, the publishers seem to be primed to get the short end of the stick.

Given that the CRB mandated royalties were by most accounts too low, and given that the labels were loath to reduce what they had already negotiated for, and finally that the streaming services didn't want to pay out more total then they were already paying out, this left huge pressure on the DSPs to fight against any publishing increases that the CRB might consider. As you might remember from the chapter on sync uses, it is standard for a film or TV producer to pay equal amounts to the label and publisher to use a song and recording in a program (i.e., a 50% / 50% split of the total music fee) whereas in streaming the value differential typically has the label getting from 5 to 15 times what the publisher gets. You can imagine that if record labels and their artists are getting 6/7ths of the pie while publishers and songwriters are only getting 1/7th, it has created a situation where two groups that would ordinarily be on the same side advocating for the value of music as used by music services are now at odds with each other.

UH, I'D STILL LIKE MY MONEY....

Let's get into a little bit more detail. As many consumers move away from an ownership model to an access model, record sales drop, and thus so do the mechanical royalties from sales which would have otherwise been paid to the publisher and songwriter. And unfortunately, as of yet the revenue lost from sales has not been fully compensated for by the increase in streaming revenue, which is far less per stream than one receives for an actual sale. Remember that on a sale, the purchaser owns the product, 9.1¢ (or 1.75¢ per minute or fraction thereof if the song is over five minutes long) goes to the publisher, and the purchaser gets not only ownership of the copy, but the right to listen to it as many times as she wants for the rest of her life. Whereas if your song is on a streaming service, while it may be available to the entire world to listen to at will, maybe no one ever will.   It is an apples and oranges comparison. What is a single "listen" to a song worth compared to ownership and unlimited listening? Seemingly a lot less.

The question often asked is how many "listens" does it take to make something equivalent to what a publisher makes off of a sale? I took a look at the actual earnings data at my own company. As expected, the income categories reported by each DSP varied. For example, Apple is via paid subscription only whereas Spotify has both paid and free tiers. Some DSPs have phone carrier bundles, student discounts, family plans, etc. while others didn't.

In an effort to make as best an apples-to-apples comparison as possible while presenting the data in a reasonably digestible way, I excluded certain sub-categories that were not consistent across DSPs (cloud locker income, lyrics, reduced rates for families, students, trials, carrier bundles, etc.), and then grouped the remaining income categories into two parent categories: paid subscription and free ad-supported streaming. The income analyzed was from the October 2018–March 2019 periods across all clients' statements received. Client earnings were of course grossed up to 100% in cases where we received < 100% for comparison.

Note, finally, that these numbers only reflect the mechanical component and do not include any performance royalties paid via the PROs.   I also included a "how many streams will it take to earn $1,000" column for both the free, ad-supported tiers and the paid subscription tiers since these micro-micro-pennies can be difficult to otherwise get a handle on.

	Subscription Per Stream Mechanical Rate	Ad-Supported Per Stream Mechanical Rate	Subscription Streams Needed to Earn $1,000 in Mechanical Royalties	Ad-Supported Streams Needed to Earn $1,000 in Mechanical Royalties
Pandora	$0.0018798137	$0.0013202752	531,968	757,418
Spotify	$0.0002802357	$0.0000445330	3,568,425	22,455,270
Apple	$0.0006168721	n/a	1,621,082	n/a
Amazon	$0.0037439153	n/a	267,100	n/a

This chart should be used as a rough idea only, as many variables are involved and my own findings may be different from other publishers. For comparison sake, it takes 10,990 CD or DPD sales to earn $1,000 in mechanicals. For example, then, you need to have 1,621,082 subscription streams on Apple to make the same money you would have made on 10,990 CDs. So, in this Apple example, 147.5 subscription streams equals what you would have made by selling only a single DPD or CD of a song.

Whether or not the service makes its revenue from subscriber fees or ad sales, there is still the fundamental underlying question of how much of the collected revenue should actually go to cover the cost of the product it is selling: music. And for mechanicals, it isn't a free market economy between a willing buyer and seller that has determined how much that should be.

THERE'S SOMETHING HAPPENING HERE: THE MUSIC MODERNIZATION ACT

The battle lines have been drawn between publishers, record labels, and artists on the one hand, and the services on the other. Music creators are looking to make up money from lost and cannibalized record sales and are using new and exciting tools to expose their songs to new listeners. Music services are looking to have songs be legally and simply available to them to exploit at fees they feel they can afford. (The services would ideally want their revenues to be as high as possible and their product costs [music] as low as possible.)

After much back and forth between industry groups representing songwriters and publishers, performing rights organizations, labels, and streaming services, a multi-party consensus was reached. No one was entirely happy with the agreement, but each party got enough of what they needed to have the agreement get the support it needed from a broad multi-interest coalition. On April 25, 2018, the House of Representatives passed this agreement in bill form as the Music Modernization Act (H.R. 1551), which was passed by the Senate and then signed by the president on October 11, 2018.

The Music Modernization Act (MMA) comprised five main areas of clarification and change:

Section 115 Reform: The MMA provides for the creation of a Mechanical Licensing Collective (the MLC) to be funded by the streaming services. The MLC will create a central public database listing all songs, songwriters, and publishers, and then be able to issue blanket licenses covering all songs in the database to any streaming service that wants such a license and complies with the law. The MLC eliminates the need for services to serve the "notices of intent" that were previously required for each and every song and use, simply get a single license, and make a single accounting and payment for the songs they streamed. The MLC would then pay the registered publishers. The MMA also provides for audit rights so that the accountings rendered by the services may be verified as accurate.

An additional benefit of the MLC is that it will receive all the pending and unmatched revenue from the streaming services that is now just sitting there unpaid. Publishers will then be able to identify and claim their share of the pool by song title, which some have estimated to be hundreds of millions of dollars.

In July 2019, the U.S. Copyright Office officially designated the industry-consensus Mechanical Licensing Collective (MLC), created by U.S. music publishers and songwriters and backed by many trade organizations including the NMPA, as the entity which will be tasked with licensing and administering rights under the Music Modernization Act.

Willing Buyer/Willing Seller: Section 115 of the Copyright Act provides for a compulsory license with rates set by the Copyright Royalty Board (the CRB). The MMA will now allow the CRB to consider willing buyer/willing seller rates when determining the compulsory (mandated) music rates. (No one ever tells GM what they can charge for their cars.) Previously, the CRB could not consider free market conditions, and the consensus in the publishing and songwriting community was that the rates they arrived at did not reflect actual market value. The sense is the publishers will be able to justify the appropriateness of higher rates to the CRB in the future.

The CRB is made up of three copyright judges and sets rates for successive five-year periods. For the 2018-2022 period, the CRB heard from industry groups and ruled that the publishers' rate for on-demand subscription services like Spotify and Apple Music will increase by 43.81% over the term (allocated between mechanical and performance components.) Clearly, they agreed that publishers and songwriters were vastly underpaid and entitled to a raise. Unfortunately, Spotify, Google, Pandora, and Amazon appealed this ruling, an act which NMPA president David Israelite called an "act of war" on publishers and songwriters, and the result of that appeal remains pending at publication time. Apple Music did NOT file an appeal, however. If the appeal is dismissed, then the increases will be retroactively payable.

Consent Decree Judges: As discussed in the Performance Royalties section, ASCAP and BMI are governed under "anti-trust" consent decrees. GMR and SESAC are not so governed and thus, have a competitive advantage over the former societies in that the rates they charge can be freely negotiated according to market conditions. The MMA changes how the judges overseeing the consent decrees are picked in cases where ASCAP and BMI cannot reach an agreement with broadcasters or streaming services and are dragged to federal rate court for a judge to hear the case. Previously a single judge was assigned to all of ASCAP's rate court cases for life while another single judge was assigned to hear all of BMI's rate court cases for life. The MMA now requires a rotating panel of judges to hear consent decree issues so that each case gets a fresh look without judicial prejudice derived from prior hearings.

Rate Setting Improvements: The rate court judges tasked with setting ASCAP and BMI's royalty rates under the consent decrees can now consider what the services pay to record labels, and other relevant information. On the sound recording, record label and artist side of the equation, a uniform rate setting standard is now applied, and the rates for pre-existing services like Music Choice are no longer considered under a separate standard, which typically results in lower royalty rates.

CLASSICS and AMP Acts: The CLASSICS section of the MMA brings federal copyright protection to sound recordings made before February 15, 1972, which were previously only protected by a patchwork of state and common laws rather than federal law (like the underlying musical compositions copyrights are). This historic lack of federal copyright protection for pre-1972 sound recordings led some streaming services like Sirius XM and Pandora to attempt to avoid paying for their use. Record labels and artists were forced to file lawsuits, and, as a result, hundreds of millions of dollars in settlement fees were ultimately paid out to record labels and artists. With appropriate letters of direction, the AMP section allows producers and engineers to collect performance royalties directly from SoundExchange when the recordings they contributed to are broadcast online or via satellite instead of the more cumbersome and error-prone process of collecting from the recording artist or record label.

HERE, THERE AND EVERYWHERE

In Europe, generally, music is being distributed (both by streaming and access models) from a centralized location, meaning that centralized (or "Pan-European") licensing and distribution of royalties is becoming the norm. Pan-European licensing is typically digital only and usually doesn't cover local-only licenses. It just doesn't make economic sense for a music company to have 12 or 14 different sets of European infrastructure for distribution, nor does it make sense for there to be a corresponding royalty distribution facility in each such territory. This results in a lot of competition between entitles like IMPEL (an English rights collection agency) and SACEM (a French rights agency) that want to be the one to collect, commission, and distribute this rapidly growing revenue.

OTHER COMPULSORY AND STATUTORY USES

In April of 2012, the RIAA (representing record companies), NMPA (representing music publishers), and DiMA (representing digital media companies) reached a compromise agreement amongst themselves as to what they felt would be a fair agreement on various rates for new license types. This framework was subsequently reviewed by the Copyright Royalty Board, approved, and then incorporated into law.

The adopted settlement provides statutory rates for the following, as summarized in an NMPA press release:

- Mixed service bundles (for example: a locker service, limited interactive service, downloads or ringtones combined with a non-music product such as a mobile phone, consumer electronics device or Internet service)

- Paid locker services (subscription-based locker providing on-demand streaming and downloads)

- Purchased content lockers (a free locker functionally provided to a purchaser of a permanent digital download, ringtone, or CD where the music provider and locker have an agreement)

- 'Limited offerings' (subscription-based service offering limited genres of music or specialized playlists)

- Music bundles (bundling music products such as CDs, ringtones, and permanent digital downloads)

What those rates are, how they are applied, and how they are calculated are extremely complex and run 44 single spaced pages, well beyond what can be included and explained in a "plain and simple" guide. In fact, many of the services for which rates and compulsory licenses now exist have ultimately proven to be insignificant sources of income or not viable in the marketplace. Nonetheless, if you're interested, the full settlement can be found here:

http://www.loc.gov/crb/motions/parties_motion_adopt_settlement_041112.pdf

I TUBE, WE TUBE, YOUTUBE

YouTube, a service started by three former PayPal employees and now owned by Google/Alphabet, has been one of the most successful websites making music and other content available to the general public. Initially, it was intended for individuals to upload short videos to a public platform that could be shared with friends, family, and the world at large. Because the content was "user generated," meaning that it was supplied and uploaded by YouTube users and not by YouTube itself, YouTube was able to avail itself of what is referred to as "safe harbor" protections. If someone uploads a copyrighted work to YouTube, and it turns out to infringe upon copyrighted material like a song, YouTube, provided it follows certain rules set forth in the Digital Millennium Copyright Act (DMCA), has no liability for the infringement because YouTube itself did not put the infringing material on the site. Rather, the infringing material was put on the site by the end user, so the uploading user has the ultimate liability for the infringement.

Obviously, though, there are exceptions. If a politician makes a campaign video using an unlicensed song and it is seen by millions of people, the damage to the publisher and songwriter could be immense. Likewise, if a company posts a product commercial using an unlicensed song, there could also be significant harm and financial liability to the publisher and songwriter. In most cases, though, the infringing uses tend to be more benign, like your Aunty Fanny singing "McArthur Park" to her cat Tony. The uploading infringer has what lawyers call "small pockets" and has not really caused significant damage to the copyright, so it is often more trouble than it is worth to go after the infringer (and often perceived negatively by the public to the songwriter/publisher's detriment).

There is a mechanism whereby publishers and other copyright owners can send a "take-down" notice to YouTube and have the infringing material removed from the site. Once YouTube has been served such notice that they have (unknowingly and with "safe harbor" protection) facilitated the unauthorized distribution of copyrighted material on their site, then there is knowledge on their part, as well as future liability, and so they want to get it down as quickly as possible. In most cases, once a take-down notice has been given, YouTube removes infringing material from its site within a day or less. Take down notices can be given through this page: http://www.youtube.com/yt/copyright/copyright-complaint.html

Over time, media companies and savvy individuals realized that it could be useful to upload material to YouTube on a commercial basis. Perhaps, for example, Paramount Pictures has a film trailer that they want the world to see. Put it on YouTube! Likewise, corporations like CBS and companies like Vevo (a joint venture of Sony Music, Universal, and others) and Hulu post content for public consumption. People and organizations who have so-called "channels" are also considered to be premium content. A well-known recording artist might also elect to create her own "premium" channel to make money off of people watching all the videos and concert clips she has made. The uploader of premium content enters into an agreement with YouTube under which they promise that they have permission to upload any copyrighted material, and undertakes to hold YouTube harmless from copyright infringement claims for the content posted.

YouTube (Google) makes money off of uploaded content by showing advertising on the site itself, or on so-called pre-roll advertising (ads you have to watch before seeing the content you want to watch), or even advertisements superimposed on top of the videos. The more people want to see the material which has been uploaded, the more money YouTube makes.

For material which has been posted, and for which music copyrights have been incorporated (and rather than submitting a take-down notice), publishers can also elect to be paid for the use of the user uploaded video by sharing in the advertising revenue YouTube collects. This process is called "monetization." YouTube would rather cut you in on the action than have to remove the videos from its site. While the major and mid-size publishers typically have direct "monetization" deals with YouTube, the easiest way for a small or independent publisher to share in the ad revenue for user uploaded videos containing their copyrighted songs is through the Harry Fox Agency, which has a YouTube opt-in monetization program. When someone uploads a video of Aunt Fanny singing your song, you would typically get around 35%-50% (14% - 18% if she's lip-syncing to someone else's copyrighted recording) of the ad revenue that YouTube makes. Most of the time this won't be huge, but if the link goes viral and 300 million people watch Aunt Fanny, you could be in the bucks. And she could cut you out of her will.

When a premium provider of material uploads copyrighted material, they are *supposed* to make a deal with you that gives them permission to upload this material, and hopefully compensates you for allowing them to do so. In many cases, this permission is buried within recording agreements ("we can post promotional videos on Vevo"), but often doesn't say anything about how they will share any money they happen to make on such internet "promotion." Oftentimes, too, premium content posters will just post your material without actual permission, and hope either that you will never show up asking for money or otherwise that you won't send an actual take-down notice. Or if you do show up, then they'll work out some settlement with you. There is a gross degradation of respect for intellectual property, both because of the high costs of enforcing rights and low level of damages to be caused, and many such premium content posters simply take the risk that their liability and exposure just won't be that much. Plus, they make a lot of ad revenue that you're not going after them for because they'll tell you 45,000 people watched your clip, and they only made $38.45, so what are your damages? But meanwhile, they've aggregated 2 million videos that have each made $38.45 and they've made $77 million.

QUE SERA SERA, WHATEVER WILL STREAM WILL STREAM

Which services will take hold with consumers and what the eventual payoff for publishers will be is anybody's guess. To me, it seems like the most likely future scenario will involve a strong presence of subscription services, and that music publishers' take of the overall pie will move closer to, or be equal to, what the record companies are currently getting.

SUNDRY USES

The main types of licensing and income we have just explored—mechanical, streaming, performance, and synchronization—comprise the most important and common areas of interest for the majority of music publishers. In the meanwhile, this chapter surveys other common types of licensing and their normal terms and conditions.

ADVERTISING

By far the most important type of sundry music license in today's market is advertising. There are many songwriters and publishers who eschew advertising altogether, many who embrace it wholeheartedly, and some who allow it only under specific circumstances. Those parties who do not wish to use their songs in advertising frequently cite the fact that the songs they create have special meaning and importance to them, and that they don't want to pervert that meaning by using songs to sell products. Some of these principled writers have turned down millions and millions of dollars. I personally have witnessed a client decline a $22 million (publishing and master) five-year worldwide multimedia advertising campaign, solely because the writers and publishers did not want to be in the business of selling "big gas-guzzling cars."

More often, songwriters and publishers who have been reticent to allow the use of their songs in commercials slowly move toward acceptance of advertising licenses when compelling reasons can be given to override the basic objection. Such reasons might include a song's use in marketing environmentally "green" products and services that help humanity. Recently one of my clients, who would previously rather have died than issue an advertising license, agreed to do so because, in that particular case, the commercial would indirectly help more than 30,000 workers to retain their jobs. Another similarly situated client, for whom advertising licensing had been unthinkable, was willing to allow the use of an important copyright in a commercial for solar energy products.

Finally, there are those who either are not so emotionally attached to their songs, or feel that having the song in the public's mind and ear might help their careers—or at least their checkbooks. Certain artists have indeed used advertisements to help propel or revive stalled careers, or simply exploit and enjoy renewed public exposure. Songwriters such as Sting, Michael McDonald, and Steve Miller have publicly acknowledged the benefits from advertising campaigns featuring their music.

There really isn't a right or wrong response to an advertising request. This is a subjective issue that's affected by, among many other things, financial pressures and realities.

The most typical advertising campaign license request is for a national (United States) one-year TV campaign. Typical fees (and there are many cases where fees are not typical) for such a campaign are in the $150,000 to $500,000 range (just for publishing). Unknown songs might even go for less than the $150,000 floor. Newer songs might be in the $150,000 to $250,000 range, with well-known songs fetching more than $250,000. For important songs that a company desperately wants to use, the sky is the limit, with possible fees well into the millions. Determining factors are the size of the company doing the advertising and the likely campaign budget, frequency of exposures, the unique suitability of the song to the product or campaign, and the desire of the advertiser balanced against the reticence (if any) of the songwriter and publisher. There might also be additional media (such as radio, print, and website) advertising thrown into the picture, and those media would raise the quoted price typically by 10% to 30%.

Advertising agencies also try to negotiate lower music fees by limiting the TV commercials to "spot television," "regional television" (example: only five western states), or "13-week advertising cycles." Fees for this nature of advertising are more likely to be in the $75,000 to $150,000 range. Granting this type of license is not without risk, though. Once you've done it, you have associated your song with a product or service. People don't know that the use is only on a spot, regional, or limited-term basis, and this license may very well preclude other advertising opportunities that otherwise may have come to light. If a song has been sitting around for two decades and no one has yet wanted it for a commercial, go for it. On the other hand, if you receive inquiries about a specific song's availability for advertising every few months (one of the first things they always ask you is what else the song has been used for and when), then it might be prudent not to knock out a big national spot in favor of a low-budget or short-term regional oil and lube commercial.

Recently, too, pricing on internet advertising has increased substantially. More and more media advertising buys are being directed to the internet, and as standard TV viewership and delivery via streaming and mobile devices increases, so too does the value of advertising over those media. Internet is the new TV! So make sure that your quotes for internet advertising correspondingly increase as you are pressured to lower your TV advertising quotes. It's all the same advertisement, it's just how it is being delivered now that is changing.

For a worldwide deal, the fees discussed above might be doubled. There is also an acceptance within the advertising industry that certain products carry a stigma, and that the fees discussed previously for these particular stigma products might be double, triple, or even higher compared with the fees discussed above. Such stigma products might include beer, hard liquor, feminine hygiene products, dog food, kitty litter, toilet paper, condoms, hemorrhoid or rectal itch products, prescription drugs, etc. *Parody lyrics,* where the song's original lyrics are changed to better suit the product or campaign, can also raise the fair market value of an advertising license by 25% to 50% or more.

Licensing for radio advertising alone, for one-year campaigns, will more likely be in the $60,000 to $120,000 range, but again is subject to many of the factors discussed above.

Outside of the United States, at least in major industrial nations such as Japan, England, Germany, France, Scandinavia, Spain, Australia, and Italy, fees for one-year campaigns related to major products and well-known songs are typically in the higher end of the $35,000 to $100,000 range (just for publishing rights), but the original publisher's local subpublisher is a good source of information concerning normal local terms and rates. European subpublishers, in particular, are more likely to tie the fees into a percentage of the total campaign budget (including media buys), frequently around the 5% figure. However, this pricing shortcut doesn't really take into account that once a song is used with a product, it is "used" in the marketplace and already has a public product association. Therefore, a low-media buy campaign done on a percentage basis might underprice the use.

THAT SONG SOUNDS FAMILIAR

One of the shameful current trends in advertising is to use knock-offs of popular songs without paying the creator of the original work. For example, if an alcoholic beverage company wanted to use a DJ Khaled song because he's hip and trendy and has lots of street cred, and if DJ Khaled wanted more money for the use than the company was willing to pay, the company might hire a writer or company to create "original" music that sounds and feels exactly like DJ Khaled's song, but which could pass a musicological exam with the verdict that it was a "different" song and did not infringe upon the original. In many cases (and in our hypothetical example), the instructions to "create something that sounds like DJ Khaled" are given verbally, and not in writing, and without any traceable paper trail. No one wants to leave a paper trail of their bad faith intent.

The knock-offs typically take lots of elements and mix them up or invert them or change the key or something clever like that. If someone was getting instructions for a Beatles sound-a-like, they might be instructed to "do harmonies that sound like those in 'Paperback Writer,' give me horns like in 'Good Morning Good Morning' and weird backwards kaleidoscope-y stuff like 'Being for the Benefit of Mr. Kite,' a guitar that sounds exactly like the one in 'Day Tripper,' the drum build up from 'Back in the USSR,' then take the melody of 'Eleanor Rigby' and mash it up with the melody from 'Polythene Pam,' only inverted and with a minor E chord instead of a major." And voila, instant Beatles. (Or Rutles.) And without it actually being the Beatles.

The artist/writer/publisher often hears about these knock-offs through website contacts, phone calls to management ("Hey great commercial for Spazzo beer"), or from fans and tweets. Nothing that happens out there really flies under the radar any more. There's always someone willing to fink on a competitor who is using music without paying for it ("Did you guys license a song to Dorkco?"), or who is thinking that no one "on the outside" will ever know about their little internal corporate video, which suddenly went viral. Trust me, it all comes out eventually if someone is trying to get away with something.

In many cases, the creators of these sound-a-like songs are either starving musicians that would do anything for money, even to the extent of ripping off other songwriters and artists, or otherwise are hired by a handful of shady and/or amoral businesses that cater to providing musical knock-offs under a veil of corporate protection, only to fold and declare bankruptcy if and when they are sued. But even if the creator disappears and has no money, the "deep pockets" usually still remain with the advertiser who used the infringing work.

Often the knock-offs get away with it. Enter the words "advertising rip offs" in Google or another search engine, and you get "about 196,000,000 results." In most cases the original creators don't want to go to court, which requires a big commitment of time, money, and energy. Only a handful of the companies that create or use the rip-offs are ever actually sued because it is such a hassle to go after them. And even if it is obvious to you that you were ripped off, it might not be obvious to a judge who thinks you look like his brother-in-law whom he resents because he hasn't worked a day in his life but wrote one hit song when he was 22 that has floated him ever since. But when a songwriter, publisher or musical group is sufficiently pissed off, or ready, willing, and able to stand on principle, the fireworks begin.

First, a musicologist is called in to transcribe and compare the new and original work. Frequently, and sadly, a musicologist has already been retained by the creator of the new work, who has already "blessed" the new work as being sufficiently different from the original so as to likely be defensible in the event of legal action. So it often becomes a case of musicologist against musicologist, expert against expert. Even if the musicologist representing the original copyright concedes that the chords and melody are completely different in the new work, the argument can still be successfully made, and the complaint can still prevail, if there exists such a collection of unique and disparate elements from the original material, that the combination of such elements cannot be a mere coincidence, but rather a calculated attempt to mislead the public to believe that the creator of the original work is the creator of the new work. Then the lawyers for the new song argue that your "unique" elements aren't really that unique, and that they are all really based on what is called "prior art," and in fact, you're the guy who actually ripped your hook off from "Venus" by the Shocking Blue and you didn't write it yourself.   "Your stuff wasn't original in the first place" becomes their defense against having ripped you off. But in legal actions where a jury is deciding a case, it is often patently obvious to the lay person that someone was trying to trade on someone else's song, type of songwriting, or musical style no matter what the musicologist for the defendant says.

VIDEO GAMES

In the past, the fees being offered by video game companies were often insulting. Manufacturers relied on the fact that the video game market is a prime demographic for a young audience that would hopefully lead to music sales, and that publishers and record companies would clamor for the exposure offered to that market for almost no money. For a while, it worked. Big games like the Grand Theft Auto series often offered buyouts in the $5,000 range. But publishers started looking at initial shipments in the range of 4.5 million units for $60, and started wondering if higher fees weren't in order.

Many of the games today, especially music-oriented games like *Just Dance* and

Rock Smith, may be willing to pay anywhere from 1.5¢ to even 5¢ per game on occasion, with significant advances. Some writer/

musicians are even ending up in the games as characters, or with their own special "expansion packs" or versions of the games. Further, some of the games now offer sell-through opportunities for players to buy the music in the game right then and there, often rewarding them with the opportunity to get additional upgrades or codes to advance in the game.

But sales of video games are diminishing, or done on a free or subscription version, and the once unshakeable belief that music sales could be increased through key demographic exposure in games is now flagging. Publishers are constantly riding a wave of paradigm shifts.

PRINT

Printed sheet music, songbooks, and album-matching folios comprise the bulk of the written music sold in the United States. There are only a few companies left in this segment of the market, among them Alfred Publishing (which acquired Warner Bros. Publications but which now has some of its repertoire distributed by Hal Leonard), Hal Leonard Corporation, Cherry Lane Music Company (which is distributed by Hal Leonard Corporation), and Music Sales Corporation.

Advances are common, and may be based on either a period of years or a number of albums. A typical advance for a matching folio for a newly released CD is in the $3,000 to $35,000 range, with new groups and talent more likely to be at the lower end. Songbooks of guitar gods seem to get good advances. Major artists with deep catalogs can attain very large print advances.

The royalty rates offered are pretty much the same everywhere, and as long as you insist that your rates are on a most favored nations basis, you'll be fine. Typically, the MFN rates are as follows:

- 20% of the suggested retail selling price of each piano/vocal sheet music.

- 15% of the suggested retail selling price of other individual sheets (easy piano, piano solo, guitar, etc.).

- 10% of educational, band, choral, and multi-artist books (*Best of the '60s, Justin's Favorites from the '90s*, etc.). Expect to be prorated by the number of songs in multi-artist books.

- 12.5% of songbooks such as personality folders (e.g., *The Best of the Doors*) and album-matching folios (The Doors, *L.A. Woman*). It is also standard to add an additional 5% royalty for the use of the artist's name, image, and likeness (*NIL royalty*). So if you, the publisher, have these rights to grant, throw them in. If the project is a Barbra Streisand or Celine Dion album-matching book, and you only control the songs and not Barbra or Celine (does anyone, really?), then you can't grant this right and won't get the 5% NIL royalty.

- 75% of net receipts from third-party sublicenses. An example is when your print company licenses two lines from your song as a chapter-heading epigram in a novel.

There may also be special provisions for lyric-only editions, unbound editions, etc. Generally, these are not economically significant and as long as you proceed on a most favored nations basis, you'll be no worse off than anyone else.

Annoyingly, there are a huge number of companies that are distributing either lyrics, or music and lyrics, of copyrighted works via the internet, either without valid license and permission to do so, or with tenuous claims to having such legal right. Go after the big ones when you can, but it is the wild west out there and you might not get much satisfaction when you discover an infringing company.

Finally, remember that the print companies are all themselves now becoming more active in downloadable and online sheet music sales. An authorized printed music agent has a good stake in helping you to stop unauthorized distribution. Royalties payable for electronic distributions are generally based on revenue sharing as the initial cost in creating the file for a given song is minimal, and as the incremental distribution cost is practically nothing. Some publishers are demanding 75% or more of the net revenue for electronic distributions. The paradigm is changing, so keep your eyes open.

RINGTONES

Programmable telephone ringtones are a meaningful but somewhat diminishing source of income for music publishers, with millions in annual fees paid. Unfortunately, a huge percentage of the ringtones sold are not authorized by the artist, publisher, or master owner. Any publisher who feels like a little self-torture should enter his biggest song title into any search engine followed by "ringtones," and he will find thousands of sites offering his song as a ringtone, many of them for free! The original cell phones often played monophonic or polyphonic versions of the song, but today the standard is almost universally "real tone" or "master tone," meaning that in most cases, you're not listening to a cheesy Casio-organ-like version of "Light My Fire," but actually hearing the famous Doors master when your phone rings. Because the record companies that control the desired masters are the sole distributor of those masters, these companies have essentially become mass aggregators and licensers of ringtones.

As of October 3, 2008, the Copyright Royalty Board set a statutory rate of master-tone ringtones of 24¢ per unit. Prior to that date, the typical rates charged by publishers were the greater of 10¢ per song, or 10% of the amount charged by the ringtone provider. In the past, performing rights societies also have collected public performance income for ringtone uses. It is also advisable to enter into these new technology licenses on an experimental, non-precedential basis.

KARAOKE

Karaoke licensing has been around longer than ringtone licensing. There are a lot of sleazy companies in this field, so be careful. These licenses are nonexclusive, so you can license to lots of different (reputable) companies. Since karaoke involves lyric reprints, make sure that your karaoke agreement doesn't conflict with any rights you have granted in a print deal. Normal or typical terms that you want to have on a most favored nations basis are:

• Term: 7 years.

- Territory: World excluding Japan (JASRAC will collect and pay your subpublisher a lot more than you'll get here in the United States).

- Royalty rate: 14¢ a unit for the first 3.5 years; 17¢ a unit for the second 3.5 years.

- Advance: 5,000 units at 14¢ = $700.

- Fixing fee: Non-recoupable additional fee of $350.

As with ringtones, you can also drive yourself crazy by entering your song titles followed by "karaoke" on any search engine. It's just too expensive to take action against someone in Taiwan whose server is located in India.

FOREIGN TRANSLATIONS

Publishers are frequently approached by foreign writers and publishers interested in doing foreign-language versions of a song. I have seen very few of these versions ever pay off for my clients, even when the group doing the foreign adaptation is "huge" in its territory. And in the few cases where a foreign version does become economically successful, there are almost always myriad problems that pop up with royalty collections, improper credits, and local regulations that eat up any benefit that you might have gotten in the first place. My knee-jerk reaction these days is to tell them, "Write your own damn song and leave my client's song alone. My writer does not need you to create new German lyrics to his hit song."

In the event my publisher client nonetheless wants to proceed, I generally do not approve of versions where only the original melody is retained and the new lyrics relate to a completely different subject than the original ones. I prefer that foreign-language versions of songs be, as much as possible, direct and literal translations of the original sentiment expressed, with reasonable allowance for local idiom. Some other terms and requirements to consider:

- The new lyrics should be a work made for hire (which means they are completely owned and controlled by the original publisher), so you are not gaining a co-publisher, co-writer, or partner in the song's ownership by permitting the new version. The copyright in the new version (a derivative work) should be in the same name(s) as the original song.

- Generally, the translator/adapter should not receive any writer or publisher share of the income on the new version (and never on the original version). Exceptions might be if you yourself commissioned the translation or adaptation, or when a superstar such as Andrea Bocelli wants to adapt your song in Italian, or Celine Dion wants to do a French version, or if a bona fide Japanese superstar wants to redo a song that flopped for you in the United States. In cases like that, where an artist brings a huge potential audience of record buyers to the table, it is a fair trade-off to grant a small but reasonable adapter's or translator's share (10%-15%?) in the newly created version only. It is almost always a nightmare distinguishing which version of the song (the original or the translated one) is earning the income, so you may simply decide that the translator/adapter gets nothing. (It's your choice.) In many cases, if the guy doing the translation is also in a group that is recording the new foreign version and is making artist royalties anyway, it won't be a big deal to him.

- Mechanical licensing should be at the full local rate.

- The new translator/adapter should indemnify the original writers and publishers against any third-party or infringement claims in case something he added to the new version of the song wasn't his to add.

- There should be a written and signed agreement that specifies your local law for venue and disputes.

- There should be a specific requirement that the new lyrics are not offensive, defamatory, or profane, or that they do not in any way demean or lessen the value of the original copyright.

- If the song is a split copyright, the permission should be contingent upon the translator/adapter receiving permission from your co-writers or co-publishers, and on the same terms, prorated.

Sometimes people may want to create same-language adaptations of your existing copyrights, such as a parody version of "My Sharona" called "My Bologna." This is almost the same situation as a translated/adapted foreign version, and you should use the same considerations in arriving at a decision on whether to approve it, and at what terms. They may argue that they don't even need your permission due to "fair use" considerations, which are discussed in the momentarily following "That's Not Fair—Or Is It?" section. The bottom line in either foreign or parody version instances should be: "Is it good for the song?"

SAMPLES

Sampling (the interpolation of existing copyrights into new ones) also creates derivative works. Sampling may involve both songs and master recordings, and where it does, the sampler requires both a master sample license and a composition (publishing) sample license.

Most sampling requests come from the rap, hip-hop, and R&B worlds. When considering a sample request, it is important to obtain and review a transcription of the lyrics or rap in order to make an informed decision. The decision of the original publisher is binding but also entirely subjective. The sampler might only be using three of your notes, or four of your words, but if those three notes or four words comprise (in your opinion) the bulk of what is good or important about the new song, you might require 80%, 90%, or more of the new derivative copyright to be owned by the original publishers. As another example, if your song comprises only a musical bed for completely new (and acceptable) lyrics, you might feel a 50%/50% split is fair. Again, the issue is completely subjective.

Most sample licensing involves joint ownership of the newly created copyright, and often an advance. If the sampling party is subject to a controlled composition clause in his recording agreement, the mechanical rate payable to the sample also has to be addressed, not just the percentage claimed of the new work. Sometimes sample licenses are also done on a flat-fee basis.

Sampling license agreements should always be in writing. They tend to be very long and complex and are often subject to our Law of Inverse Effort. (If you get into a dispute, gangsta rappers can be the wrong people to have pissed off at you. I once was asked to send a "cease and desist" letter to a rapper who was in jail for murder.) The sampling agreement should always attach as an exhibit a CD or electronic file serving as an audio demonstration of how you have agreed that your copyright will be interpolated into the new work. If you don't do this, greater or different portions of your work than you thought you were licensing might end up in the new work. Make provisions, too, as to what will happen if someone else samples the newly created work (embodying your copyright) into a third work such as a new recording or synchronization use (a new recording sampling a recording that already has a sample in it). I have started issuing sample licenses for use in audio recordings only (and maybe a promotional video too).

My learning experience was through licensing a famous chorus of a hit song published by my client to a new artist who had alternated that famous chorus with his own original rapped verses and for which my client agreed to a 50%/50% split on the new song. Well, when a major car company came along and wanted to make an advertisement using only the chorus from the new song (i.e., the only thing they were using from the new song was my client's famous chorus and they were not using any of the new rapped verses), I was put in the situation of being asked to consent a 50%/50% split of $350,000 with the author of the new verses. Of course, we had retained the legal authority to not agree to this, but this serves to illustrate why I like to withhold newly excerpted segments (as opposed to whole song uses) of works embodying samples of my clients' works in sync uses and other new derivative works. The same thing applies to synchronization uses of songs that contain samples. You should retain the right to re-evaluate the shares of sync uses as the portion of your song used in the sync use might be much greater (or smaller or the same) than it was in the overall audio recording.

Always make sure that there is an indemnification in favor of the original writers and publishers against any third party or infringement claims for new material added to your original work. If you are only a co-publisher of the sampled work, you should require that your co-publisher also agrees with the proposed use and terms.

THAT'S NOT FAIR—OR IS IT?

Special attention and further research might be in order for those particularly interested in sampling and parody. Recent court decisions have effectively carved out *de minimus* (minor, in legal speak) uses as not requiring sample clearance. Further, §107 of the copyright act provides for certain types of *fair uses*, for which no license or permission is required. For example, if I am writing a scholarly book about the '60s and the war in Vietnam, and I want to include an analysis or criticism of Neil Young's song "Ohio," which is about the National Guard's killing of four antiwar protestors at Kent State, I can legally do so (as long as such use of the lyrics falls within fair use constraints). Free speech trumps copyright law. Copyright law (§107 again) is not intended to stifle free speech, and specifically states that fair use "for purposes such as criticism, comment, news reporting, teaching (including multiple copies for classroom use), scholarship, or research is not an infringement of copyright." So if you want to quote and mock bad song lyrics in a review, you can.

The four factors that are listed in the statute as to what constitutes fair use are:

- The purpose and character of the use, including whether such use is of a commercial nature or for nonprofit educational purposes.

- The nature of the copyrighted work.

- Amount and substantiality of the portion used in relation to the copyrighted work as a whole.

- The effect of the use upon the potential market for or value of the copyrighted work.

What this all means is that you now have a bunch of rather (well, let's be blunt) murky and independent conditions and factors that the courts get to interpret (or misinterpret, depending on the case). There's plenty of case law on this, much of it with narrow meanings that people want to apply broadly to their own benefit. Fair use claims and defenses thus require great care and understanding.

NEW TECHNOLOGIES

New technology is developing at a blistering pace. I keep talking about paradigm shifts. When I tell my kids that there were no color TVs, ATMs, e-mail, texts, smart phones, GPS, microwave ovens, Internet, DVD players, video games, apps, personal computers, or tablets when I was a kid (and I'm not that old), they look at me like I came from a different planet. (Yeah, and people hadn't walked on the moon yet, and there were only 48 states.) There are already competing new home audio formats, SACD and DVD-Audio. As I write, Neil Young continues to work on high resolution delivery of sound recordings on his "archives" website. And nobody seems to want ownership (as opposed to subscription access to anything) anymore anyway. And Dad still has 3,000 12-inch vinyl LPs in the closet, which are now cool again.

Bearing in mind, therefore, that some details in this book may be obsolete before it gets into print (disregard all the numbers or double them!), how do you deal with whatever new technologies come sailing across your little copyright world? Safe advice is to let others go first. Why should you be the guinea pig? I had a client who gave his songs (practically for free) to a music game app developer, only to have the developer sell his game off six months later to a huge entertainment conglomerate for $35 million, of which my client got nothing but the chance to help someone else make a fortune. Once you see what works for others and what doesn't, and who has been burned and how, then you can jump in. But that caution could also prevent you from enjoying a great opportunity before the rest of the world catches on.

You can protect yourself by making short-term most favored nations deals for new technologies that you can get out of if the archetype takes a rapid twist on you. Long-term deals for developing and emerging technologies can be dangerous. Try to keep the new technology license form on a well-worded most favored nations basis with all other music publishers. It should also be deemed to be experimental and not prejudicial to any future position on how future licensing will be handled for any further use of the given composition, or for any other compositions.

These protections and reservations allow purveyors of new technology to progress, while simultaneously providing protections for the music publisher and assurances that if industry standards or statutory law improves upon the current business model, the licenses too will advance correspondingly.

SUBPUBLISHING

Subpublishers represent publishers and their repertoires in foreign territories. Some music publishers, mostly the multinational companies such as Warner/Chappell, Sony-ATV/EMI, Universal, and BMG, own and operate their own subpublishing offices in various territories throughout the world. While this is an advantage for the companies, it may not be an advantage for the company's clients.

Most publishers employ subpublishers in various territories of the world. Canada is usually, but not always, excluded from subpublishing coverage for United States publishers because of its proximity and the ease of dealing directly with Canadian companies from the United States. (If you're a music publisher in New York, for instance, you're probably a closer distance to a Canadian record company than to a record company in Los Angeles—and Canadians are friendlier.) Some music publishers hire one multinational firm to represent them throughout the world. Others go on a territory-by-territory basis, hiring the best subpublishers they can find in each territory.

In actuality, each country of the world does not need to be covered. There are many countries of the world where either (practically speaking) copyright obligations are not recognized, or where the income deriving from music copyrights is so small that the cost of collecting your money is higher than what you would get. Many countries are assembled into more manageable territorial groupings. It is thus possible to cover most of the world by having between 15 to 20 subpublishing deals in place. Setting up and maintaining this number of deals can be a lot of work. However, there are clear advantages to picking the best subpublisher in each territory as opposed to making a deal with one preassembled grouping, which may have weaker offices in one country and stronger ones in another. Having individual direct deals also maintains a direct sense of accountability and responsiveness to the original publisher, while dealing with one central office does not.

The following are the most typical groupings:

- Australia, New Zealand, Fiji Island, and the trust territories of New Zealand (Papua, and Western Samoa).

- The United Kingdom of Great Britain, Ireland, Northern Ireland, Scotland, and Wales, and PRS territories excluding Canada, Australia, and New Zealand.

- South Africa, SAMRO territories including Botswana, Lesotho, Transkei, Bophuthatswana, South-West Africa (Nambia), and Swaziland.

- Belgium, Netherlands, Luxembourg, excluding Radio Luxembourg and Radio Europe #1.

- Spain and Portugal.

- Sweden, Norway, Denmark, Iceland, Finland, Estonia, Latvia, and Lithuania.

- France, SACEM territories excluding Luxembourg but including Radio Luxembourg and Radio Europe #1.

- Germany, Austria, and Switzerland.

- Poland, Czech Republic, Romania, Bulgaria, Slovakia, and Hungary.

- Italy and Vatican State.

- Japan and Mandate Islands.

- Greece.

- Mexico.

- Far East, including China, Hong Kong, Singapore, India, Thailand, Korea, Taiwan, and Malaysia.

- Israel.

- Argentina, Uruguay, Chile, Paraguay, and Bolivia.

- Brazil.

- Russia.

- Slovenia, Croatia, Albania, Bosnia, Herzegovina, Serbia, Macedonia, Kosovo, Montenegro, Moldavia, Malta, and Cyprus.

- Turkey.

(If you are particularly interested in how UK music publishing works, there is a UK version of this book that focuses on how copyright and licensing works in the UK.)

A GOOD SUBPUBLISHER

Music publishing, as a field, is filled with intricacies and complications. The best music publishers are well suited to dealing with myriad details, deadlines, and regulations. Organization, efficiency, and attention to detail; strong mathematic, verbal, and negotiation skills; honesty; and dependability are among the most important characteristics of a music publisher. So, too, are these the qualities to look for in a subpublisher. It also helps if the subpublisher communicates well in English, if that's the only language you know.

It has been said that a good subpublisher is one who answers your letters, phone calls, and e-mails quickly. While there may be some truth to this adage, it is important to remember that the correlation between speed of reply and subpublishing quality is not one of causality but one of association. Efficient businesses are on top of things and deal with the tasks at hand promptly, but forcing a poor-quality subpublisher to answer correspondence within 24 hours of receipt doesn't make its fundamental weaknesses go away. So look for speed of response, but also look deeper.

One of the best ways to find a good subpublisher is to talk to other music publishers. The size of a subpublishing operation is not necessarily important. Further, some publishers prefer independently owned and operated subpublishers. Multinational companies are in business both as publishers and subpublishers, and they might take a fancy to one of your catalogs or songwriters. There are situations in which your subpublishing service provider might turn out to be a competitor, and you should take this possibility into account.

LET'S MAKE A DEAL

Making a deal with a subpublisher is generally easy. Most foreign countries have far less of a legal culture than the United States, and usually you will be negotiating with the subpublishers themselves and not foreign lawyers.

The typical initial term for a subpublishing deal is three years, with extensions thereafter in one-year increments. The smallest music publishing catalogs might attain an 85%/15% split with a subpublisher. In really small territories where revenue is minimal to begin with, you might even enter into an 80%/20% deal. Large, more significant catalogs will get a 90%/10% split, and extremely important and prestigious catalogs may even get a 95%/5% split. In general, these splits apply to all types of income. Cover recordings and foreign film and TV placements solicited by and secured through the subpublisher's own direct efforts are generally rewarded with higher splits. Money that is earned *but uncollected* in foreign territories by the original publisher is also referred to as *black box* (or *suspense*) *income* and eventually gets distributed to all the publishers whose works were properly registered and collected in that territory as a kind of bonus. So if you wait too long to make a subpublishing deal, your earnings will go into the *black box* fund and someone else will get them. It is much better to be the recipient of unallocated black box income than a contributor, and depending on your clout, you may be able to get a subpublisher to agree to pay you a proportionate share of the black box income he receives.

If advances are being given by the subpublisher against future earnings, the split is usually between 85%/15% and 75%/25%, and the performance split may be doubled so that the subpublisher is getting an imputed commission on the writers' half of performance income (which is paid directly to the songwriter and does not pass through the subpublisher's hands). Where advances are taken, it is also typical that the agreement has automatic one- or two-year post-term extensions if the advances given are not earned out at the end of a typical initial three-year term. So your three-year deal might end up as a five-year deal if it doesn't earn out. Ironically, this rewards poor collection.

Many territories require that foreign taxes be deducted from your earnings before your subpublisher sends them to you in the United States. Among these are Italy, Spain, the Far East (varies by country), Australia, and New Zealand. Usually, the amount is no more than 10%, and you should expect to get a tax certificate at the end of the year that may get you tax credits on your United States income tax return. Check with your tax professional. Other countries allow your income to be paid to you without any local tax deduction, although you may have to fill out exemption request forms, and such forms might have to be signed by your bank, certified by the Internal Revenue Service, or accompanied by documentation provided to you by the Internal Revenue Service. Your subpublisher should be able to help you get this going much quicker than your accountant can because of much prior experience in these matters.

Subpublishers are usually empowered to issue full-rate mechanical licenses and to collect local performance income. The normal subpublishing agreement, though, requires approvals from the original publisher on all advertising, synchronizations, samples, and translations or adaptations within the territory. Rights not explicitly granted to a subpublisher should also be reserved to the publisher. It is common that synchronization licenses (subject to the foregoing approval requirement) for films and programs originating and produced within the subpublisher's territory, may be issued for not just the local territory but for the world.

Finally, make sure you don't focus too much on the split of a proposed subpublishing deal and too little on the quality of the collections and reputation. A 10% commission with one company hardly ever results in the exact same net income to you as a 10% commission with a different company. And 75% of excellent collections is a lot more than 90% of poor collections. This point was brilliantly illustrated to me a few years ago when I switched from an 85%/15% deal with a multinational subpublisher covering South America, which had been producing a few hundred dollars' income per year, in favor of an 80%/20% deal with an independent that immediately paid out more than $10,000 on its first rendered royalty statements. There's always someone who will do it for less, but that doesn't mean you'll get more.

AN EXPERIMENT GONE WRONG

Focusing on percentages instead of subjective qualities can also get a publisher into trouble in other ways. Many publishers have attempted to bypass subpublishers altogether and (where possible) collect directly from the foreign end music user, or directly from the foreign mechanical or performing right society. Since the local subpublisher is getting 10% of the money that he is getting from the local society, why not simply cut out that middleman and collect 10% more? In many territories, this practice is not prohibited by local law, and it is possible for a publisher to become a direct member.

I tried this some years ago in England (figuring there would be no language barrier) and obtained miserable results. The unfortunate xenophobic truth is that people give more attention and care to their own countrymen than they do to someone who doesn't know the local ropes and is separated by 6,000 miles and a ten-hour time difference. My conclusions were that paying a small sum for a subpublisher's local expertise is a good thing (penny wise vs. pound foolish) and that local law and custom are best dealt with by those operating in the territory and possessing the specific local knowledge and clout to get difficulties fixed, explained, or sorted out. Knowing how to work the local system and authorities (knowing who to bribe and when . . . just kidding!) is probably worth every cent you pay to an honest and hardworking subpublisher.

By way of analogy, think of a laboratory where you're mixing chemicals together through the use of robotic arms behind double sheets of bullet-proof glass. It is much harder to do the job this way than if you could just pick up one beaker and pour the chemicals with your own two hands. The process takes a lot longer to do by remote, and the chances that you might spill something are much greater. Trying to do your subpublishing from "behind the glass" is quite similar.

Let's say that your direct collection agent doesn't actually have a representative in a given territory, and some local company wants to use one of your works in a major advertising campaign and they contact the local mechanical or performing right society. If you're unlucky, they can't find your representative and you lose a big opportunity. (I saw this happen last year with a former client whose new direct collection agent had no local representation in Argentina.) If you *are* lucky, that society, in turn, refers them to the direct collection agent in some other country. Then you have to hope that the advertiser is (hypothetically) able to communicate well in a different language through different time zones and has enough deadline time that he doesn't give up on his quest to use your song. You also have to hope that the direct collection agent has (or can get) appropriate information about how big the potential advertiser is, what a typical fee is for that territory, and close the deal in the foreign territory. More robotic arms. Is it really worth saving 10%?

You could also save big on your medical bills by going to WebMD, self diagnosing yourself, buying online prescription meds from India, and self-treating. But is it really worth saving $150 on that doctor's visit when he could have taken one look at you and told you you have Argyria? Be careful how much you save. It can and will cost you big.

As a final side comment, in general, if you're looking to collect the fruits of your livelihood through a new publicly financed company using fundamentally unsound and/or untested business models, you should probably read their annual report closely to learn more about them.

THE SUBPUBLISHER DINNER CIRCUIT

If you live in a major United States city and/or if your publishing catalog is significant enough, your subpublisher may come to visit you and other American clients every year or two. Recognizing the importance of maintaining personal relations while doing business at great distances, a very large number of subpublishers travel to the United States annually to meet and greet you or even to pitch you on their representation (if they don't work with you already). Face-to-face meetings with a great number of subpublishers in a short period of time are also possible at the MIDEM convention, now held each June in Cannes, France. And if you are lucky enough to be able to travel to a subpublisher's city and country, you are likely to receive a warm welcome, fine hospitality, and accompanied local tours and sightseeing. One of my favorite aspects of the music publishing business is the genuine friendships that have developed with people in other countries and cultures, and the opportunity to travel to, know about, and feel comfortable in many areas of the world outside of the United States.

CO-WRITING AND CO-PUBLISHING

It is common practice now for more than one writer to collaborate on a song. If you review the writer credits for the songs on the Billboard "Hot 100" or "Hot R&B/Hip-Hop" charts, you will find many instances of four, five, or more writers and publishers (and that one asshole from the record company) listed as writers on a given song. (And try to find any Hot 100 songs written by one, or even two writers!) While some of these entities might be included due to incorporated samples, group collaboration is undoubtedly an important songwriting method these days.

It's important to understand how a song comes together and how publishers and their songwriters protect and legally handle the jointly created work. As we discussed previously, copyright exists once a song has been fixed in a tangible medium from which it may be reproduced. When there are two or more writers, in the absence of a written agreement to the contrary, copyright law deems that the split between the writers is equal, and makes no attempt to determine who contributed what and how important their contributions were. Except for nearly minimal contributions such as suggesting a title or changing a word or two or a note or two, each party is treated as the equal owner of an undivided interest in the song. When two writers collaborate, each owns a half of the whole song, even if one contributed only the lyrics and the other only the music. When three writers collaborate, each one owns a third undivided interest. When four writers collaborate, each one owns a fourth undivided interest, and so on.

So-called "top-liners" are brought in to polish up a song. In reality, top-liners are people who can actually write a catchy melody and/or good lyrics, and who are brought into a project to make a bunch of junk that everyone else has been mucking around with into a half-way decent song. But of course, the "muckers" will still want a good-sized piece of the song that wouldn't be worth anything without the top liner.

It is important for the writers to agree *when* the work is finished (when it has been fixed) because at this moment in time, several important concepts and rules kick in. If you and your co-writers are working on a song and you have to take a break for a few days, you all need to agree that the song isn't finished yet and is still a work in progress. Once the work is finished and has been recorded in some format, it becomes a *joint work,* which in copyright speak means that you have the intention that your "contributions be merged into inseparable or interdependent parts of a unitary whole." Think of it as a musical latte. Once you add the steamed milk to the coffee, you're not able to separate it out again. On the other hand, if the work has *not* been finished, it is more like a soft drink with ice in it. You can take the ice out and use it elsewhere if you want.

From the time a work is finished, further changes to the song have all sorts of ramifications and may even be prohibited by law if one of the writers does not want them. Such changes (to create a new song, version two, based on the first song) would constitute the creation of a derivative work, and if unauthorized might actually constitute copyright infringement. If this were not so, then your co-writer could effectively force you into collaborations and co-ownership situations with people you wouldn't want to collaborate with or perhaps had never met.

These rules lead to some possibly counterintuitive results. Let's look at a few examples.

If you collaborated equally on the lyrics with someone but wrote all the music, in the absence of a written agreement between the two of you to the contrary, each of you own half, even though you may feel as if you have done three-quarters of the work. There is no "separate but equal" concept with respect to music and words. As far as the copyright goes, you are equal creators of the joint work.

Here's another example. Let's say you finished a song with two co-writers, and then your co-writer, Bob, decides that the lyrics in the verse you wrote suck and wants to replace them with his own.

Bob cannot do so without your permission, because that would constitute the creation of a derivative work based on the jointly completed, fixed copyright that had been created by the three of you. If you ultimately saw it Bob's way and agreed that your lyrics were actually bad and agreed to allow the removal of all of your contributions and lyrics in favor of new and improved ones by Bob, you could nonetheless lay claim to a one-third share of the new song, because you were a one-third owner of the finished song upon which the new work was based. This also gives you the power to prevent your contributions from being stripped out or altered from a finished work without your permission. Likewise, this prevents the dilution of your interest by the addition of more writers after you and your original co-writers have finished the song.

Obviously, fixing your finished work in a media (and thus stopping the clock on the creative process) could be an important step before you bring it into a recording session. Otherwise, the song could get "refinished" in a recording session or band rehearsal, and you could find yourself with four new claimants who decided or remembered that they helped you finish the song. Paranoia about this sort of thing can be bad for collaborations, but a laissez-faire attitude could also leave you with six co-writers you never met. Bands working out songs together must have a clear internal understanding about the distinction between songwriting and simply working out a bass and drum parts for your song. It is best to talk openly about this up front, and, if possible (I know, this is the music business), to collaborate only with those who you feel are aboveboard and honest.

It is very common for writers (especially outside writers) to think a song is finished and recorded, only to have a producer or label bring in new people without your knowledge to do further work on it, and then expect you to reduce your share of what you thought was the finished work. Strictly speaking, they don't have the legal right to do this, but if you make a fuss and don't reduce your share so that the asshole A&R man at the record label can get 10% of the song for adding the word "The" to the song title, you might not get called back by said asshole to work on future projects. It's a slippery slope.

BACK TO REALITY

In reality, not everyone contributes equally. The copyright law's provisions are what take effect when you don't bother to decide among yourselves. It's kind of like dying without a will. When you don't make a will, the government will decide who gets what for you. If Joe the drummer only contributed a little bit to the song, you and Joe need to arrive at an agreement that his share was (for instance) only 20% and that your share was 80%. If you don't make this agreement, then the copyright goes automatically to the default 50%/50%. This type of agreement should be in writing but need not be complex or fancy to accomplish its basic intent. It might be written on a napkin or scrap of paper and say something as simple as, "On March 1, 2004, Joe D. Rummer and Bob DeGuitar finished a song called 'Whoo Hooo,' and the share of ownership is agreed to be 20% to Joe and 80% to Bob. [Signed Joe and Bob]." Sometimes the writing members of a group give a piece of the writer and/ or publisher share to the non-writing members just to keep them happy and to reward them for their other non-songwriting efforts like touring to promote the song. Remember, though, that this is a gift and not an entitlement, so you should proceed carefully.

DON'T BOGART THAT JOINT (WORK)

OK, so let's say that you are now the proud 25% co-owner of a fixed joint work and copyright. In short, you now co-own the music publishing on the song, and you need to know what you can do with it. In the absence of a written agreement by the other three writers (or their designated publishers) to the contrary, you are free to license the work on a nonexclusive basis without any permission from your co-writers or co-publishers. While you legally have the right to grant nonexclusive licenses on behalf of 100% of the copyright, some potential licensers of the song will nonetheless insist upon obtaining licenses from your co-publishers for their shares of the song.

What types of nonexclusive licenses can you grant without the other co-owners' permission? Provided that the song has already been publicly distributed, you can issue mechanical licenses for the whole song. (Since a first mechanical use can only happen once, it can be argued that a first mechanical use is an exclusive type of license.) Likewise, you can also grant nonexclusive synchronization licenses for the song to be used in TV shows, films, advertising, ringtones, sheet music, etc. The logic behind this provision of the law is that if one owner that has a chip on his shoulder or is in a feud with the other writers, he will not have the ability to prevent the others from enjoying the fruits of their labor by holding up the licensing.

Co-writers and co-publishers issuing nonexclusive licenses on behalf of 100% of the song do nonetheless have obligations to the other writers and co-owners. They must take steps to ensure that crediting on these nonexclusive licenses includes all writers and publishers. They also have specific legal requirements including the obligation to account to the remaining writers (or publishers) for their rightful shares of the license fees.

Co-writers and co-publishers do not have the right to issue *exclusive* licenses on behalf of the whole song. Such prohibitions include the exclusive right to use the song in advertising (where you explicitly agree that you will not license the song for any other advertisements during the license term), the exclusive right to print sheet music of the song, the exclusive right to subpublish the whole song (although you could grant your subpublisher the right to subpublish *your share* of the song), or the exclusive right to use the song as a television theme song. Any time you would like to issue a license that precludes your co-writers or co-publishers from issuing a license to someone else for the use of a song, it is *exclusive* in at least some aspect, and you (and the would-be licensee) thus require the consent of the co-publishers. That also means your co-writers and co-publishers can't issue an exclusive license without *your* consent, which protects your property as well.

Think about the ramifications of this. Your 10% co-publisher cannot exclusively license 100% of the song to his uncle, the president of Coca-Cola, for $100, in all of Coke's worldwide advertisements. He could do it nonexclusively, but you would not then be precluded from approaching Pepsi-Cola and nonexclusively licensing 100% of the same song for Pepsi ads. It would be unlikely and even foolhardy for Coca-Cola to enter into a nonexclusive license to use the song in an advertising campaign that would cost millions of dollars if the company knew its rights were only nonexclusive and faced the possibility of someone else using the same theme song in other commercials. Practically and realistically speaking, the distinction between nonexclusive and exclusive licensing, and the rules about who can issue these licenses, protects all parties well.

Finally, in the absence of a previously agreed prohibition, even though you do have the legal right to issue nonexclusive licenses on behalf of the whole song, it is not a very nice thing to do to your co-writer or co-publisher. It is preferable, where possible and where all the writers are still speaking to one another, to discuss the terms and conditions of a proposed nonexclusive license, and to make the decisions mutually and in good faith. Licensing the whole song by yourself ought to be a last resort, like when your co-writer is in the Himalayas and forgot his cell phone and you "know" he'd be OK with it and you'll lose the opportunity if you don't do it without him. Oh, and by the way (you don't get off that easy), even if you do issue a nonexclusive license on behalf of the whole song, you still have a very specific obligation to account to and pay your co-writer/co-publisher his or her share of the license fee.

Even though potential licensees know that they could legally get a nonexclusive license from only you, they may not necessarily feel comfortable doing so. For example, what if they got a nonexclusive license from you to use the song on a TV show as a background vocal at a high school dance, and then your famous co-writer turned up and gave an interview to *Rolling Stone* where he talked about how much he hated that sitcom and how he never would have issued that license and what a rat you are? You can see why, where possible, licensers like to have all owners and writers on board. When they are desperate (the program airs in four hours and they have only gotten approval from one of the four publishers), they might go the less nice (but nonetheless legal) route.

LET'S MAKE MORE PAPER

When there is a reasonable likelihood that a collaboration will have significant exploitation, it is often advisable to have an agreement drawn up (a co-administration agreement) that specifies ownership, control (administration), and other important terms.

The most important function of a co-administration agreement is to list the writers and their percentages of the joint work. If the writers have assigned their works to publishing companies (even their own), the agreement lists the publishing companies and their respective shares as well as all of the parties' respective addresses. The agreement provides for registration of the work in the U.S. Copyright Office according to the given terms and splits.

Administration of the joint work may be handled in several ways, and the chosen method is specified in the co-administration agreement. If one party is administering the whole song for the others (this would more likely be called a co-publishing deal then), the agreement states that and lists and defines the obligations (accounting, obtaining approvals, clearing works with performing right societies, defending against infringements, etc.) that the administering party has to the other writers and publishers. More commonly, if all parties are actually able to administer their own shares of the publishing rights, the agreement specifies that each party will directly administer, license, and collect their own respective shares only (including via their own respective subpublishers), and that each party is accepting an affirmative obligation to inform potential licensers that they must contact the co-publishers to obtain licenses for the remaining shares.

In addition to normal contractual provisions (such as venue and choice of law, cure periods, and breaches) co-administration agreements should also contemplate:

- The treatment of print rights (especially important if one or more of the writers already has a print deal).

- Controlled composition clauses (especially if one or more of the writers has or might have a record deal that subjects him to a controlled composition clause).

- Under which circumstances, if any, a reduced-rate mechanical license will be granted.

- The process for dealing with requests for derivative work licenses (samples, parodies, medleys, etc.).

- Promotional video rights in the event that one or more of the writers is also a recording artist who is likely to release promotional or concert videos.

- The accounting of inadvertently received moneys whereby one of the co-writers (or co-publishers) receives all of the money for a given license and not his respective share.

- Warranties that each party's contribution to the joint work is original and non-infringing, along with related indemnifications.

- The defense of claims against one or more of the co-writers and co-publishers with respect to the work, and the determination of when, if, and how to prosecute claims concerning the song against third parties.

- The sale of a party's respective interest, including possible matching or first-refusal rights.

CONTROLLED COMPOSITION CLAUSES

Controlled composition clauses, also referred to as "firstborn male child clauses" (at least as far as music publishers are concerned), are among the most detested parts of a typical recording artist agreement. Publishing mechanical royalties are usually paid from the first record distributed and are not usually subject to recoupment of any advances or recording costs. Because the license fees represent immediate out-of-pocket costs, the record companies like to do everything in their power to reduce and limit their amount and delay their payment.

A CONTROLLED WHAT?

The first part of any controlled composition clause is the definition of a controlled composition. Since the record company will eventually get around to asking for a reduced rate on controlled compositions, it behooves them to define what they are reducing as broadly as possible. Ideally they would like a controlled composition to be something like "any song you may have written or ever heard," and then they would like you to give them a discount on the mechanical rate to be charged for such song. Realistically, controlled compositions are more likely to be something like "any song written or co-written by you, or any song owned, controlled, or administered by you." They will also endeavor to require that you agree that any musician, producer, engineer, arranger, etc. that you hire to work on your records also agrees to be bound by the terms of the clause. So not only do you have to get screwed, but you have to agree that you will require everyone else you work with to get screwed too.

If you are a recording artist and songwriter, and if you *already* have a publishing deal with a company, it is very important to ensure that a deal you are making with a record company does not conflict with the terms of the publishing deal and does not have you granting rights to the record company that are not yours to grant. Conversely, when making a publishing deal, it is important that the publishing company you are dealing with is aware of and accepts any controlled composition terms that you have agreed to in a recording agreement, which will result in a significant drop in income to the publisher (i.e., the ability to recoup advances they are giving to you).

THE METER IS RUNNING

The first thing that enters into the controlled composition rate is the date upon which the reduced statutory rate will be based. In a perfect world you would receive a full statutory mechanical rate that "floats"—that is to say, a rate that is subject to future increases in the statutory rate. The first thing record companies want to do is stop the clock. Actually, they want to turn it back. Specifically, what they try to do is fix the mechanical rate basis even before the date the record is released and maybe even before the song was written. The wording in the controlled composition clause thus states something like: the mechanical rate is based on "the earlier of the date that you turn in the record, or the date that you were contractually required to turn in the record." The idea is that they would like to pay you based on the statutory rate that was in effect before its last increase and even before the date your record was released.

Since United States mechanical rates change every few years, the chances are good at any given time that a statutory rate change is near. Delayed releases are extremely common due to remixing, recording of additional songs, availability in release schedules, additional up-front time required to set up the initial release (preparing videos, ad campaigns, etc.), the record company firing that asshole A&R man who signed you, and coordination with live performance tours. So there can be a long (or at least longer than you'd probably like) lag between the time you turn in the record and when it actually comes out. Further, since the label reps pick an arbitrary due date upon which you are required to turn in the record, they argue that just because they were nice enough to let you turn in your record two years late, why should they suffer and pay a higher mechanical rate than they would have if you had it delivered on time? If possible, you should try to have the controlled composition mechanical rate be the one in effect on the date of release.

OUR SPECIAL REDUCING FORMULA

The next thing that a controlled composition clause does is to reduce the rate that will be paid in as many ways as possible. The record company tries to have a clause with wording that says you will (typically) get a "mechanical rate based on 75% of the fixed minimum statutory rate." As discussed above, the label will also try to take steps to ensure that the statutory rate it is paying you 75% of is last year's model. Two words, here, fixed and minimum, will also prevent you from enjoying eventual increases in the statutory rate and from enjoying any long-song payments.

Since record company greed, like most other forms of corporate greed, knows no bounds, the controlled composition clause will also try for further reductions in the rate by giving it a definitional name such as "Your Mechanical Rate" and then proceeding to list various circumstances and types of additional reductions that can be taken with respect to Your Mechanical Rate.

For instance, the label will try to obtain rate reductions for lower price configurations. Perhaps, "mid-line" units (i.e., those sold for less than top-line, full-priced releases) might be paid at 75% of Your Mechanical Rate, and "budget" releases at 50% of Your Mechanical Rate. So you are now looking at 75% of 75%, or even 50% of 75% of the fixed minimum outdated mechanical rate. Labels will also attempt to specify that they are only required to pay these mechanical rates "on royalty-bearing units." Elsewhere in the agreement, "royalty bearing units" will be defined to exclude things like "free goods" (discussed in the mechanical royalty chapter), "special free goods," "promotional copies," and anything else they might be able to think of. So with 15% taken out, they will now be paying you 85% of Your Mechanical Rate, again with configuration reductions (where applicable) as discussed above. Are you sick yet?

The types of reductions record companies think of seem boundless. Because the controlled composition clause might read to the effect that "you hereby license 'controlled compositions' to us for use on phonorecords" at the specified rates and terms, you are not just licensing your shares of these songs, but all of your co-writers' shares as well. Because of this "you are hereby licensing" wording, they will also take the position that the recording agreement constitutes a license in and of itself, and they don't need another piece of paper to explicitly license any of the controlled compositions to them. This means that they are effectively calculating the rate themselves, and that because you or your representative is not issuing an actual license to them, you often will not know (let alone agree with) what rate they are paying until they've begun accounting to you. Lastly, because you are licensing the controlled compositions to them "for use on phonorecords" *as opposed to for use on specifically identified phonorecords*, they may even get the opportunity to turn the clock back further in the future. When you release a live album, a best-of album, or a greatest hits album, you may well find that they have the right (according to the controlled composition clause) to pay you for the use of the controlled compositions not at the rate in effect at the time of the new release, but at the rate in effect for when you first "hereby licensed" the song to them on your flop first album eight years ago.

JUST IN CASE THAT ISN'T ENOUGH

In order to ensure that you aren't as sneaky as they are, record companies have also introduced the concept of an aggregate mechanical cap. What would happen to the record companies if recording artists actually wanted to give record buyers more value by putting, say, 15 songs on an album? Well, they'd have to pay mechanical royalties on these songs. Or, heaven forbid, what if an artist turned in a record that had 30 two-minute songs on it? To guard against this possibility, the record companies have come up with an aggregate mechanical cap that typically runs from ten times

Your Mechanical Rate for baby bands to 14 times Your Mechanical Rate for superstar acts.

To see how this works, let's say you're in a mid-level band and you have a 12-song cap. So you multiply Your Mechanical Rate (which may already be hugely reduced, as discussed above) by 12, and that is all the money that the record company is obligated to pay you for mechanical royalties. But you have 14 great songs and you want to put all of them on your record. Penalty time! Since you have already agreed that the label has to pay you at most 12 times Your Mechanical Rate, and since your maximum mechanical rate pool only covers 12 songs, you have now effectively agreed to a further 12/14ths reduction of Your Mechanical Rate. Ha ha! You lose!

But there's more. Let's say that you didn't write all of the songs on the record. Let's say you've done a cover recording of Bob Dylan's "Lay Lady Lay," plus another song you were lucky enough to co-write with Mick Jagger, and a third song you wrote with your brother-in-law who isn't in your group and isn't subject to your recording agreement. Dylan's music publishers, although they are very nice, don't see why they should accept your controlled composition rate (they get no benefit from your recording agreement, after all) and regretfully insist upon a full, floating, long-song statutory rate on all units made and distributed. Mick Jagger, too, figures that he is entitled to a full rate for his half of the song, even if you have agreed to accept Your Mechanical Rate for your half of the song. Your brother-in-law, though, is someone whom you can browbeat to share the suffering. (He no doubt deserves it and you'd enjoy it. Why should he make more for his half of the song than you make for your half of the song? So go ahead!)

Thus, before any mechanical rates can be calculated for the songs on the record, you have to reduce your allocable mechanical rate pool by the full current long-song (where applicable) statutory rate times 1½ songs to pay Dylan and Jagger. Then you get to allocate the remaining money, which for argument's sake let's say amounts to 10½ times Your Mechanical Rate (it may be less because Dylan and Jagger might be paid at the long-song current statutory rate, and your aggregate mechanical cap might be based on an older noncurrent rate). You now take this 10½ times Your Mechanical

Rate pool, allocate it over the 12½ songs written by you and your controlled brother-in-law (i.e., 14 songs total less Dylan's song less Jagger's half song), and you are thus left with each of your songs getting 10½/12½ of Your Mechanical Rate, which is worse even than the 12/14 reduction of two paragraphs ago. (Dylan and Jagger are used only hypothetically here, and their respective publishers may have different positions and reactions than we've attributed to them in this illustration. Or they may not.)

Since you've "hereby licensed" the whole song, you have to be particularly cautious about the treatment of your co-writers. If they don't agree to be "controlled" (i.e., to go along with your controlled composition rate, terms, and payment methodology) and insist upon a full rate, that amount will come out of your aggregate mechanical pool, making you in effect pay the differential between your co-writer's share of a full floating long-song statutory rate and your co-writer's share of Your Mechanical Rate, thus even further reducing the mechanical pool allocable to your songs (and your brother-in-law's too).

Some controlled composition clauses are kind enough to anticipate that there might be a few "outside" songs, and may have a separate mechanical pool allowance for payment of full floating statutory payments for such songs that does not affect or reduce the artist's own aggregate mechanical cap or pool. Additionally, some recording artists with sufficient clout, or with a proclivity toward putting out albums that contain fewer but longer songs, have been able to get *min-max* wording put into their controlled composition clauses. These clauses, while limiting the worst-case scenario to the record company (the maximum aggregate cap) conversely protect the songwriting recording artist. If such an artist has a "12 times min-max" clause but turns in an album that has ten lengthy songs on it, the proration would be reversed and might allow the artist to receive 12/10ths of Your Mechanical Rate, sometimes resulting in a greater than statutory mechanical payment. You see these min-max clauses more often in older recording agreements under which vinyl records were the primary sound-carrying media, with their limited number of songs and playing time relative to CDs.

Recording artists who write little or none of their own material might require different sorts of controlled composition clauses. Such recording agreements may even provide that the record company (perhaps jointly with the artist) gets to pick and approve the proposed song list and number of songs, and is responsible for obtaining mechanical licenses at the best rates it can, and for its own sole benefit, for all of the "outside" songs (i.e., non-controlled compositions).

ET TU, BRUTE?

Controlled composition clauses also tend to provide for reduced-rate mechanicals in Canada. (Outside of the United States and Canada, mechanical rates are rarely, if ever, reduced, and most recording agreements specify that the rates payable outside of the United States and Canada will be paid according to local rate and custom.) Many of the Canadian reductions parallel the reductions of the United States rate. Because Canada has eliminated its statutory rate, the controlled composition reductions are typically based on the "usual and customary" Canadian rate, or the rate specified under the Music Canada-CMRRA schemes discussed in the mechanical licensing chapter.

The Music Canada-CMRRA schemes have also been known to include terms that the members of Music Canada have agreed will supersede lower rates or smaller aggregate caps specified in a particular recording agreement. It is advisable to check on these terms when issuing mechanical licenses for controlled artists in Canada. By virtue of the whole-industry agreement, you might actually be entitled to a better rate than you agreed to, but only if you know about it and ask for it.

WAIT, THERE'S MORE!

Modern controlled composition clauses have even broadened the applicability beyond mechanical uses. The clauses will likely have provisions giving the record company the right to have a free synchronization license for a controlled composition if it produces a promotional music video. There might also be a "just in case" clause specifying that if you ever release a live concert DVD, you have agreed up front to what the rates on that hypothetical product will be. Record companies would like you to agree to this now, when the products are only pie in the sky and you are less likely to negotiate hard for the proper or fair rate.

New technologies such as ringtones and digital deliveries are finding their ways into controlled composition wording, and again, even though such uses may not be presently contemplated, it is important to take proper care to ensure that you won't regret what you have agreed to now sometime down the road.

NOT THINKING THAT FAR AHEAD

In a lot of cases, when copyright law is revised, one of the guiding principles in making changes is to make sure that the two parties of an existing agreement each get the benefit of the bargain they made under the laws that were in effect at that time. Prior to 1995, digital phonorecord deliveries weren't on that many people's radar. So copyright law allows pre-1995 controlled composition clauses to be used to reduce the mechanical royalty rate payable for electronic deliveries in the same manner as if those sales were physical units being sold. Each party made the agreement with the expectation of a commonly shared outcome.

However, for agreements entered into on June 22, 1995 and after, when electronic music files started coming into greater prominence, the game rules were changed. Even if an existing post June 22, 1995 recording agreement has a controlled composition clause in it, which specifies a reduction in mechanical royalties on electronic deliveries, it is not valid or enforceable and the publisher is entitled to full statutory mechanical rates on these deliveries regardless of what the parties themselves have agreed under the Digital Performance Right In Sound Recordings Act of 1995. This may subsequently be renegotiated by the parties to effectuate a reduced mechanical rate on electronic deliveries, although it is hard to imagine what inducement might be given in order to make lowering one's mechanical royalty rate palatable. The logic in coming up with this law is that there is almost no incremental cost in delivering a phonorecord electronically (while there is a significant incremental cost in manufacturing each physical unit), and that reducing said mechanical royalty rate is perhaps overzealous and predatory, and thus not permitted.

SEEN IT ALL BEFORE? OR HAVE YOU?

When writing this chapter, I did not once look at a controlled composition clause; instead I relied solely on past history and experience with hundreds of such clauses. The intention was to avoid picking on any one record company's clause, or to point out any specifically onerous points incorporated by any particular company. Controlled composition wording is continually evolving or devolving (depending upon whether you're on the record company or music publisher side of the fence). There is always someone somewhere thinking of new, exciting, and not readily apparent ways to pay less money to music publishers and to (believe it or not) downplay the importance and value of songs in the music business.

In particular, American record companies have been trying unsuccessfully for years to get away from a statutory "penny rate" (one specified in fixed cents, such as 9.1¢) and go to a percent-based mechanical royalty (such as 8% of wholesale selling price), obviously because the price used in the percentage calculation is arbitrary and unilaterally determined, and thus manipulable. (Hey, Joe, let's just call the wholesale selling price $2, and then we can charge the dealers $6 per unit for shipping and handling, eh?)

CAN YOU MAKE IT ALL GO AWAY?

You can get a de facto admission from most of the major record companies that what they are doing with controlled composition clauses is over the top if you accept their offer to make a publishing deal with their sister music publisher. Almost all major record companies possess music publishing divisions, and if you agree to make a deal with them, many record companies will agree to much more favorable terms (to you) in your controlled composition clause. To use a hackneyed phrase, this deal may be like taking from Peter to pay Paul, or like hiring the fox to guard the henhouse. The typical trade-off in such an arrangement would be to base Your Mechanical Rate on a full statutory mechanical rate, possibly even floating and not fixed at a point in time, in exchange for making a co-publishing agreement where you give the sister publishing company ownership of half of your publisher's share. Since half of the publisher's share is really only 50% of 50%, or 25% of the whole, the argument goes that by giving up 25% of the ownership, you are getting an extra 25% on your mechanical rate. And that means, the argument might continue, that while the proposed co-publishing agreement only goes for a period of years (maybe 12?), the benefit that you obtain in terms of getting a full rate will go on forever, or for as long as the company continues to sell your records.

In analyzing these proposals, you should evaluate how deeply you want to get into business with one particular company (remember our earlier 360 deal discussion). While synergy may be the watchword of the day, in this case it may just mean giving up more rights and shortchanging your own best interests. You should examine if you want one sole company to control both your master and publishing rights, or whether you want separate controls, checks, and balances. Remember, too, that if you become very successful as an artist and songwriter, you will have the clout to renegotiate your deals and terms, especially your artist royalty and mechanical rates. Record companies always want more records or tours or videos or interviews from successful artists and feel the very real necessity and benefit of keeping them happy. The clout that comes from past success (or from perceived market competition for a given recording artist's or songwriter's services) may well allow better terms in the initial or renegotiated agreement.

MORE ON COPYRIGHT

In the "Overview" we covered some of the fundamental terms and concepts of music copyright law. This chapter takes a more detailed survey of the copyright issues that are most relevant to songwriters and music publishers. For further depth or research, the United States Copyright Office provides lots of good information online (www.copyright.gov), including information circulars, text of laws and regulations, and even downloadable blank, fill-in PDF forms. There are many good books and periodicals on various aspects of this field covering a wide variety of specific topics and issues. An attorney well versed in copyright law can also be invaluable for evaluating and resolving specific situations. Unless specifically mentioned to the contrary, this discussion relates only to songs written after January 1, 1978, the effective date of the 1976 Copyright Act.

As discussed previously, your ownership of the copyright in your song exists automatically once you have fixed it in a copy or phonorecord. Nonetheless, there are advantages to making your claim a matter of public record promptly after creation, and you are precluded from bringing an infringement suit until you have made such a registration.

HEY PA, WHAT'S THIS FORM?

The PA form is used to register works of the performing arts. This includes songs consisting of words and music, or just music. There are two forms of registration, in either unpublished form (indicated by a registration number beginning with PAu) or published form (indicated by a registration number beginning with PA). Both afford you many of the same protections; the main difference is that a PAu registration protects the work even if you have not yet distributed copies or phonorecords to the general public. In some instances, a song may be copyrighted first as an unpublished work and subsequently as a published work. One advantage to first copyrighting a song in unpublished form is that you are demonstrating the song is "finished," and thus any subsequent modifications or additions constitute derivative works.

Let's say you send your song out to a recording artist to consider for her next album, and you have already submitted a PAu copyright registration in unpublished form. If she, at a later date and without telling you, writes two more verses and reworks your bridge, puts it on her album, and claims half the writing and publishing credits, you can certainly cut her off at the pass. (Of course, it would be a different story if she came to you up front and got your permission and blessing to do so.)

The current cost for a paper PA or PAu registration is $85. Alternatively, you can do it online for $35 (single application, single author, one work, not for hire) or $55 (includes everything else). Additionally, along with your payment and filled out form, you have to submit a nonreturnable copy of your work (referred to as the deposit) in the "best edition." According to the Copyright Office, the best edition is the "one of the highest quality" and fullest available recorded demonstration of the song. Your deposit may be a CD, vinyl disc, tape, written sheet music, etc. The copyright office has recently made a proposal to reinstate a group registration option for songs contained on an album (GRAM, or Group Registration of Works on an Album of Music). Albums will again be able to be registered at a fee proposed to be $75.

Anyone can register a work in unpublished form, regardless of home base or nationality. For published registrations, there are restrictions, but registration is allowed if one of the writers is living in the United States or is a citizen, or if the first commercial release is in the U.S. The date of registration is the date that the Copyright Office receives the whole package from you in acceptable form. It may nonetheless take two years or more to get the completed form back from the Copyright Office, especially if there is an anthrax scare and everything sits untouched in a room at the Copyright Office for six months. The duration of copyright runs the author's entire life plus 70 years thereafter. If you are a drug-addled loser and die when you're 28, but your songwriting partner is Mr. Healthy, the 70 years doesn't start running until he dies. Good advice is to write with people who are more talented and healthier than you are.

A mention must be made here, too, of an embarrassing problem that the Copyright Office is currently experiencing. Many music publishers are finding that the Copyright Office claims to have received the application and payment but not the deposit that was sent. Copyright Office employees have admitted to me that there is a theft problem within their ranks. If you send in a nice new $250 box set for registration, someone might just walk off with it and you might be asked to send another one. Likewise, if you send in a tape of unreleased demo songs by a superstar artist, you better hope they don't end up on eBay. It is incredibly frustrating that the parties charged with protecting your works might be stealing or bootlegging them. Always save a copy of what you are sending as a deposit. Additionally, it is unfortunately advisable that you send your whole package by a traceable method of delivery (certified mail, FedEx, etc.). If this problem doesn't get any better, you can do what I do and submit the copyright registration to the specific honest examiner known to me, after letting him/her know by phone or fax that the registration is on the way.

WAIT, I CHANGED MY MIND

Let's say you have sold, given, or otherwise transferred your copyrights (registered after January 1, 1978) to another party at some point in your career. This could be anyone from a music publisher to your brother-in-law, your ex-wife, or a tax trust. You have a legal right to terminate that transfer of your copyrights even if it completely contradicts a written transfer agreement. This termination right comes 35 years after the date of the publication under the grant. So the first possible effective termination date for copyrights registered on January 1, 1978, was in the year 2013. (And 1979 works were terminable in 2014, and so on and so forth.) There are very specific regulations as to how you serve notice that you are terminating your transfer and taking your copyrights back.

The timing of this notice has to be at least two years but not more than ten years prior to the effective termination date. Note that a transfer of ownership cannot take place until the works' creation and existence, which means that if you had a 1977 songwriting agreement, but didn't write a particular song until 1979, you can still terminate the transfer as a post 1978 work even though the transfer agreement (but not the transfer itself) was in 1977.

For older works written on or prior to December 31, 1977, the authors of such works have two five-year windows in which to terminate the transfer: either the five years prior to 56 years after the initial registration, or the five years prior to 75 years after the initial registration.

Such terminations are effective in the United States only, and do not afford you the right to recover your songs outside of the United States. Additionally, licenses issued by the party from which you have recovered your rights (or will recover your rights) may still be binding upon you, even if the term of that license has run past the date of the effective termination. In some cases, the party from which you have recovered your rights might even have an ongoing right to enjoy the fruits of licenses that party issued before you terminated its rights. You should know, too, that transfers cannot be terminated if they are part of someone's will. So if Dad always liked you better and gave you his songs on his deathbed, your sister, as the trustee of his estate, can't terminate that transfer and get the songs away from you. The bottom line is that terminations are a gift from the government, and anything you can get back is better than everything that you gave away.

There is a bitchin' termination calculator here:

http://www.wixenmusic.com/copyright-termination-reversion-calculator/

But you can see how complicated and intricate this can get in a hurry.

THE CORPORATION WROTE YOUR SONG

A work-for-hire song is written under a person's scope of employment. The results and proceeds of that work (including the right to claim authorship and ownership) do not reside with the "employee for hire" but rather with the "employer for hire." Without getting too technical, an example is if someone hires you on a work-for-hire basis to write a jingle or to score a movie. The ad agency or the studio, in these cases, is the legal author of the music and the legal owner. Unless your agreement with the ad agency or studio provides for additional compensation or royalties, your fee is your complete consideration. Work-for-hire copyright duration is the shorter of 120 years from creation or 95 years from first publication. It should be noted, too, that works-for-hire are not subject to terminations of transfer, so think really hard about what you're doing when you agree to work for hire.

I FEEL RENEWED

Songs created prior to January 1, 1978, are subject to older copyright laws and have an initial 28-year term, a 28-year renewal term, and then two additional terms (added by new laws) of 19 and 20 years respectively, for a total possible duration of 95 years. Copyrights expire at the end of the appropriate year, not on the anniversary of the registration date. Renewals of copyrights are filed on an RE form and have to be done in the author's name. The cost is $100. Works copyrighted between January 1, 1964 and December 31, 1977 are automatically renewed under 1992 copyright legislation without the necessity of filing a form.

TRANSFERS AND OTHER FORMS

The Copyright Office maintains a transfer registry. Since all copyright is initially vested to the author, and since all copyright transfers are required to be in writing (you can't just tell your manager, "Here, I'm giving this song to you," thank God), the Copyright Office must reflect a transfer if the author is not the final or eventual claimant. A transfer may be indicated on the original PA registration where you are asked to check a box explaining how you arrived at being the registered claimant ("by written assignment" is sufficient where accurate). If a transfer of ownership occurs after the initial registration has been made, the transfer documents can be recorded in the Copyright Office transfer registry as public notice that the ownership has changed. Other documents relating to ownership, liens, etc. may also be recorded in the transfer registry. The cost is $105 for the recordation of a document with one title, with $35 additional per extra song title up to ten.

A CA form can be filed to correct errors in previous registrations. The cost is $130. The Copyright Office is pretty happy to take your money for just about anything you can reasonably think of as well. For example, if you don't want to wait two years to get your form back, you can expedite the registration for $800. If you can't find a registration you are looking for, the Copyright Office will charge you by the hour to research it for you. If you'd like an extra copy of your certificate, the cost is $50. Aside from the thieves in their midst, the Copyright Office workers are generally a helpful and accommodating bunch.

CAN YOU HELP ME, SR?

Another way of registering a song is as part of a sound recording (SR copyright) registration. This can be done only in limited circumstances where the ownership of the copyrights in the sound recording and in the musical composition is exactly the same. The authorship statement in section 2 of the SR form should state that you are claiming both works. So if you and your band intend to jointly own the master recording but you are the sole songwriting claimant, this type of registration would not work for you.

THE ADVANTAGES OF BEING DEAD

If you are dead, you can't be held to performance of a written songwriting agreement after your death. This good news means that if you assigned someone a copyright and renewal rights, but then you went ahead and died before the renewal rights accrued to you, the renewal rights were thus not transferable by you. In practical terms, this means that if you died before the date that a copyright was eligible to be renewed (this is only applicable for a pre-1978 copyright), your assignee doesn't get to claim United States renewal rights—your heirs do. Now aren't you glad you died?

This benefit is different than terminating a transfer because you have to be dead to enjoy it. Make sure your heirs know that they have or might have this right, so they don't get bamboozled into reassigning the renewal right to the original publisher. If you're only near death, but some of your works will be eligible for renewal in the future, you should explain to your heirs how all this works. With respect to a 1978 and post copyright, the right to terminate after 35 years again resides with your heirs, but since there is no renewal on 1978 and post copyrights (remember, you get "the author's life plus 70 years" on these), there is no renewal right for the heirs to claim.

As we discussed earlier in this chapter in the "Wait, I Changed My Mind" section, being dead only benefits your heirs in the United States. Other copyright laws in other countries (such as the United Kingdom) may recognize the concept of reversionary interests. In order to maximize the benefit of your death in this regard, it would be advisable to seek out legal counsel well versed in international copyright laws.

THE ADVANTAGES OF BEING FOREIGN

Finally, please remember that the subject matter discussed has been oriented primarily to music publishing within the United States. (There is also a Plain and Simple Guide to Music Publishing UK Edition that deals primarily with music publishing in the UK.) Other countries have different copyright laws and customs, some of which are remarkably similar to ours and others of which are significantly different. There have been many international treaties seeking to standardize copyright protections from one country to another, and to ensure reciprocal protections of copyright to citizens of countries signatory to such treaties. Such treaties include the U.C.C. (Universal Copyright Convention, 1954) and the Berne Convention for the Protection of Literary and Artistic Works (1989).

The Berne Convention significantly includes the concept of an author's *moral rights,* which says, "Independently of the author's economic rights, and even after the transfer of the said rights, the author shall have the right to claim authorship of the work and to object to any distortion, mutilation, or other modification of, or other derogatory action in relation to, the said work, which would be prejudicial to his honor or reputation." So they can't mess with your stuff even though they own the copyright, because that would be *morally* wrong. Sadly, the United States has not amended its copyright laws to comply with this internationally recognized protection for creators, while nonetheless maintaining that it otherwise adheres to the Berne Convention. Some have speculated that this situation is due to lobbying by the United States' film industry, which desires to maintain the broadest possible rights in work-for-hire productions without any regard for rights that are "morally" (if not via ownership) possessed by the creators.

REPRESENTATION AND FURTHER ADVICE

This chapter will cover a variety of loosely related topics that warrant some discussion but are not significant enough to justify complete chapters in their own right. Consider this the free-advice section.

YOU GET WHAT YOU PAY FOR

It is often the case that newer songwriters and publishers cannot afford proper representation when entering into new agreements. It is also often the case that established songwriters and publishers don't want to afford proper representation (i.e., they hate paying lawyers). In many cases this leads to negative long-term consequences.

When hiring a lawyer, be sure to choose someone with significant prior experience in the areas that you need. Just because some guy has graduated from law school and passed the bar exam doesn't necessarily mean he knows the first thing about recording or publishing agreements, or that he has any real-world experience that will allow him to advise you about what is normal and what is not. Your cousin Vinny might be a lawyer and willing to cut you a great deal, but he might not know the first thing about a controlled composition clause. Sure, he'll look it up in some books and articles and do the research, but someone who deals with these issues day in, day out will be much more effective.

It is also likely that more experienced counsel, although costing much more per hour, will be able to finish the job in much less time. It is possible, even, that such counsel has previously negotiated with that same company and same agreement form and can get to the end much more quickly and cheaply by just saying, "Hey, can you just incorporate the changes we made in the Joe Blow deal into this one?" While each agreement is different and each client has different needs, someone with experience can get to your specifics more efficiently.

Inexperienced attorneys are (in my experience) more likely to heavily mark up an agreement to demonstrate to their clients the value of the services. Unless the client is an attorney himself, or unless he possesses genuine knowledge and industry experience, the marked-up agreement is likely to seem impressive. On the other hand, a plethora of ridiculous or inappropriate comments telegraphs to the other side that the attorney does not know what he is doing and does not understand industry norms.

Another point to consider, too, is that experience is real and tangible but clout is only perceived. If a record or publishing company is offering you a great deal, it is because *you* are that valuable. It is not because your lawyer is some big kahuna that the company reps are shocked and awed by. While Mr. Kahuna might be able to get them on the phone quicker, and might be able to call in some favors or a tit-for-tat to push over a given point, the basic value of the deal accrues to you and your talent. A bombastic lawyer or manager who brags that he got you an $8 million dollar deal did so because the company wanted you that badly, and it would have given the same deal, more or less, to anyone else who could offer your services. Don't forget that the worth of your own services is what ultimately drives any music deal.

Some attorneys and business managers like to or are willing to work on a percentage basis instead of an hourly (or by the job) basis. Typically, this percentage is around 5%. (Correspondingly, almost all personal managers work on a percentage basis.) It is therefore very important to consider how the method of compensation is likely to color a negotiation. Attorneys and managers who are receiving a percentage of your deal may feel an incentive to front-load the deal with cash as opposed to maximizing long-term benefit and revenue. These people may not be secure in the knowledge that you will want them to represent you for the long haul, and they may simply want to get decent compensation for their work now. This dynamic may lead to deals in which the up-front guarantees are strengthened at the expense of a lower and more disadvantageous split of income to you or a longer agreement term.

It would certainly be an uncomfortable situation if, deep into a negotiation, you start wondering whether the advice and representation you are getting is untainted. While tainting is a possibility in this scenario, it is also possible to receive questionable advice on an hourly basis. There is not a week that goes by when I do not see the flames of what would seem to be an easily resolved dispute fanned and made worse because someone keeps getting $850 per hour as long as the dispute is not resolved. In fact, if lawyers' hourly rates went down retroactively the longer a dispute went on, you'd see things settled and resolved much quicker.

It is also possible to put a cap on a fee for a given job ("You'll do this job for $850 an hour, but in any event you won't charge me more than $10,000"). This can limit your costs, but it can also serve to limit the amount of attention the deal gets if it runs into unforeseen problems.

So where does this leave you? It is certainly hard when you distrust parties who are supposed to have your best interests in mind. Keep your eyes open and beware of pitfalls. If something doesn't seem right, get a second opinion.

MY LAWYER IS A SEWER, ER, SUER

In the music business, there are generally two types of attorneys: transactional attorneys and litigation attorneys. In some cases, but not often, attorneys do both transactional work and litigation work.

Transactional attorneys specialize in negotiating deals and handling day-to-day commerce. For example, they might negotiate publishing and record deals, set up and maintain corporation and partnership agreements, help you negotiate deals with band members or co-writers, and work with publishing administrators on music licenses.

Litigation counsel specializes in filing and handling lawsuits and defending against them. As examples, litigation attorneys might defend against a suit in which someone claims that your song was stolen from theirs. Or these attorneys might sue the record company for failing to account to you properly. Litigation in the

United States tends to be very, very expensive and the costs (which are likely to be higher than you could imagine or project) should be carefully weighed against the potential benefits, financial or otherwise. Going to court to right a wrong, for egotistical reasons (be honest with yourself), or on the basis of principle is a luxury to be accorded only the wealthiest individuals or large corporations.

If, however, there is a genuine dispute involving more money or significance than the legal fees are likely to cost, and if you know you would be willing to take the matter to court, it is probably worthwhile to immediately retain litigation counsel and not have a transactional counsel as the lead player. The attorneys and players on the other side may, unfortunately, be dismissive of what they face when contacted by a transactional attorney. They know they are fairly free from litigation costs or any real danger until you have hired a litigator. They know that if they can't get the matter resolved with your transactional attorney, they get one more chance at settlement with the litigator you will then have to hire. In other words, they may not fear or respect a lawyer they know won't sue them. Although transactional attorneys often work for firms that also have litigation attorneys, in order for your position to be taken seriously, it may be unfortunately necessary to bring in the litigators. Sometimes you get more with a big stick; sometimes you don't. It is also highly advisable to get a trusted team together to manage the litigation approach and costs. If you let your litigator do whatever she wants without guidance or restriction, you may be paying for a lot of things that might fail the cost/benefit test.

A BOY NAMED SUE

Inevitably, and way too frequently when you have a hit song, you yourself will be sued. As soon as that money starts landing in your account, people come out of the woodwork claiming that they wrote your song and you stole it, nyeah nyeah nyeah. On a recent hit song administered by my company, I had three unrelated parties come out and say that the song was written by them and stolen. My suggestion that there be an elimination tournament whereby the three potential claimants would fight it out for the right to sue my client in a Super Suit was not met with favorably.

Almost all of these suits are nuisances, often brought maliciously or by a party playing with less than a full deck, and often banking on fears of bad publicity. Unfortunately, the saying that "every suit has a nuisance settlement value" is often true. You are often stuck with the unsatisfying choice of paying someone $20,000 to go away (without admitting any guilt) versus spending $200,000 in litigation defense costs that you might never recover even if you prevail.

In infringement suits, the plaintiff must prove both that you had access to his material and also that a substantial similarity to the allegedly infringed work exists. To eliminate the access claim, it is highly advisable not to listen to or even accept any unsolicited songs from anyone you don't know or have any doubts about. Nonetheless, access to the allegedly infringed work can be claimed or proven if the original work was publicly disseminated (for example, if it was on a well-known record or played on the radio millions of times). "Substantial similarity" (which can also be a unique combination of similar but common musical elements) will be argued by the musicologists on both sides, but in reality, both judges and juries will listen to the two works in question and make up their own minds regardless of what the experts have to say.

LET US COUNT THIS DAY OUR DAILY BEANS

At a certain level, you may want to switch from your local family accountant to a business manager. Business managers offer all the same tax and bookkeeping services that your local accountant does, but they augment it with (you hope) keener business advice, tax planning and structuring, and retirement and investment knowledge. They also handle many of the day-to-day aspects of insurance acquisition, bill paying, home and automobile purchases, etc. In any case where clients have significant income, it is important not to blindly abdicate responsibility for money and investments to a third party. Take reasonable care in selecting a business manager, and be sure to maintain oversight and awareness of your situation no matter how boring or technical it may be.

The music business is filled with people who made millions of dollars on one hit in the '60s or '70s but now struggle to get by on what little income oldies tours or their name can get them

THE PLAIN AND SIMPLE GUIDE TO MUSIC PUBLISHING

because they blew it all on drugs, cars, houses, divorces, and private jets. Likewise, there are people who had that same one hit but are comfortably living out their years in a paid-for house in Bel Air, using those modest royalty payments to pay the property taxes and put their kids through college.

A couple of specific bits of advice:

Know how much money and other assets you have and where they are, and be comfortable in the understanding that everything is in your name.

Be very wary of investing in businesses with your manager, attorney, or business manager. You want them as non-interested advisors, not as your business partners.

If your investment involves offshore partnerships and trusts, and complicated tax strategies that you don't remotely understand, make sure that you also have significant investments and assets that could support you if the complicated stuff disappears. While some complicated tax and asset management strategies are brilliant, others are simply complicated and may even be disallowed.

Sign your own checks, and review your own monthly statements. There is no other way to know what you are spending or what you have.

KNOW WHAT THEY OWE

Auditing a record company or a publishing company is one of the smartest things a recording artist or songwriter can do. Most recording and publishing contracts are written so as to limit any potential liability to the company to the amount of recovery. In other words, there is often no specified penalty or interest owed to you when you discover how much you have not been paid. The typical worst-case scenario for a record or publishing company is that they get forced to pay you the money they already were bound to pay you in the first place. While there are penalties and civil remedies available extra-contractually for fraud, most of the errors made in the company's favor are characterized as "inadvertent," "unintentional," or "subject to contractual interpretation." But then again, most of the errors do seem to be in the companies' favor, so maybe they really are just convenient mistakes?

Anyone with earnings of more than a few hundred thousand dollars over a three-year period is advised to audit a record company. Record company accounting is extremely complex and even convoluted. I have almost never seen a record company audit that did not recover at least the auditor's costs, and for this reason, it is often possible to find competent and qualified auditors willing to work on a contingent fee basis. An artist who has released four to six albums auditing a major record company over the last three years' statements (typically the contractual limit) might expect to spend $25,000 to $45,000 for such an audit, depending on the specifics. A new artist auditing only one or two albums would spend less, and an established artist with 27 albums, and four different record company accounts, obviously significantly more.

The publishing threshold for when an audit is justifiable might be higher than for record companies because publishers generally do not manufacture and distribute physical products. In fact, in the absence of fraud or intentional malfeasance, most publishing companies do a fairly good job of passing on your share of the receipts and accounting to you. Many of the potential payment shortfalls found in a publishing audit may even be apparent from the statements themselves. For example, if the publisher is supposed to pay you 75% of the income but is only paying you 67.5%, you can see that you have a problem without going in for an audit. Publishing company audits generally reveal claims of the nature of income that the company should have collected but didn't (i.e., poor publishing administration results in unregistered songs and uncollected income), or upstream commission or tax deductions that are not contractually permissible. For these reasons, it is much harder to make a publishing company audit pay off than a record company audit.

You should not worry about offending your record or publishing company by auditing them. While they hope you won't, auditing is a normal part of everyday business that they expect to deal with. Even if your account is unrecouped due to advances, an audit is advisable if there is a chance that your account might someday recoup. The proceeds of the audit, when applied to an unrecouped balance, bring you that much closer to payable balances.

LEARN ME MORE

The topics covered in this book comprise a survey of most of the important things you will need to know on a day-to-day basis. In fact, if you understand and absorb most of the content, you'll be ahead of 90% of the pack.

When things get complicated beyond the scope of the basic information presented here, there are several good places and ways to get more information, and there are people (international copyright attorneys, for example) who specialize in very specific and limited aspects of copyright and music publishing fields. As noted elsewhere, excellent information is available online through the United States Copyright Office (www.copyright.gov).

There are many good books on music publishing, and specialized aspects of music publishing, such as *Nimmer On Copyright* by Melville B. Nimmer and David Nimmer (Matthew Bender) and *Kohn On Music Licensing* by Al Kohn and Bob Kohn (Aspen Publishers).

DIY

Since the first edition of this book was released, the music industry has been decimated by a number of factors including illegal downloading, high prices, competition for entertainment dollars, and unforgivable industry greed and stupidity. The Music Modernization Act and other factors are now reversing that trend. Overall, though, it is very hard for new or marginal acts to eke out a living right now in the music business. And thus, all the parties that make a living providing services to music creators and songwriters are also seeing hard times.

Lawyers can't charge a "baby band" $20,000 to negotiate a recording contract because the band is only getting $20,000 total to sign and make a record, not $250,000 as in the old days. Managers can't afford to manage you if your record career is only generating $25,000 per year, and if you're not making significant money off of your touring. Likewise, with a top 10 album selling 30,000 copies per week instead of 850,000 copies per week, you're not going to find a publishing company willing to hand out the dough on a silver platter. And if you're not in the top 10, you might just find that the cost of collecting your money in a workmanlike manner actually exceeds the amount you have earned.

Imagine a new band selling 5,000 CDs per year at shows and via its website. This might produce in the neighborhood of $6,250 in mechanical income, and let's just guess $500 in performance income. With a straight 10% administration deal, the administrator would only make $675, which would not likely cover the time spent copyrighting 12 songs, affiliating the writers and publishers with a performing right society, clearing songs with that society, and issuing mechanical licenses to the record company.

This chapter, therefore, is intended to be a brief checklist of what you can do yourself and how to do it, as a stop-gap measure to protect your rights and your songs until you hit the big time or end up back working at McDonald's.

PROTECT THE SONG

The first thing you might want to do is copyright your songs and, if applicable, your master recordings. This can be done on a PA or PAu (unpublished works) form for a cost of $35 online, or $85 with paper. Further, if you also own the master recording (meaning that you aren't recording for a record company that owns your recording proceeds), you might be able to cover both the master recordings and the compositions embodied therein on a single SR form. The circulars that are available from the Copyright Office online are very helpful and well written.

In all likelihood, once you send off the form and the deposit (a copy of what you are copyrighting) to the Copyright Office, you won't hear back for a year or two. Right when you've completely forgotten about it, the examiner will call you to ask you a question or tell you how to correct your form, or otherwise send a letter to that effect. Don't feel bad or worry that your work isn't covered. A large number of submitted copyright forms need revision or clarification. In most cases, too, your work will be covered from the date the Copyright Office received your copyright application, even if the form does require subsequent revision or modification. If by chance the examiner has no issues with your form, you will then receive a completed copyright certificate back in the mail.

UNCLE SAM WANTS YOU,
AND SO DO ASCAP, BMI, AND SESAC

The next thing up on the agenda will be to affiliate with ASCAP, BMI, or SESAC. GMR will only be interested if you're already a top tier writer/publisher and have significant earnings or cache. Take a meeting with each society to ask them why you should join their organization, and ask them what they're going to do for you. If you don't live in a city with an ASCAP, BMI or SESAC office, you can always call them on the phone. BMI, in my experience, tends to be more helpful and nurturing, while ASCAP, though seeming to pay more, tends to be more "talk to the hand" about rules and regulations. All the performing rights societies are pretty overwhelmed with changes in the law and insane amounts of earnings data to be processed from the streaming services, and quite frankly, do a less than optimal job. Hopefully, it will get better. At the beginning you should really be more concerned with the assistance you will get rather than the money you might make someday. The affiliation will need to be done for each writer, and there also should be at least one publishing company affiliation. (If one member of the group is or wants to become an ASCAP member, and the other three are or want to become BMI members, then you will need to form at least one ASCAP publishing company and one BMI publishing company to publish the respective shares written by those members.)

Some groups take the approach that they will just start one publishing company that will publish everything written by all the group members ("All of our songs will go into Spastic Sisters Songs"). Since group members often change during the course of a career, my own preference is that each member has his or her own publishing company. It makes the eventual "divorce" so much cleaner if the community property has already been divided up.

The affiliation forms are easy and straightforward. ASCAP, BMI, and SESAC are there to help you with any questions on what to do. In addition to the applications you fill out, you will also have to sign their standard affiliation agreements. These are preprinted forms in tiny type, and for the most part, the performing right societies never negotiate what is on the forms, so you will probably want to just sign them and send them in with your applications. BMI and SESAC notify you if your affiliation is accepted, and ASCAP notifies you if the "Board" has "elected" you to membership.

Now that you are a member, the next thing will be to clear your songs with your chosen society. This means that you are telling ASCAP, BMI, or SESAC the specifics of the song or songs you have written, and is in effect your instruction on how to collect and pay out any income the song may eventually have. This process is done online now. Again, if something is kicked back to you for correction or clarification, it is a fairly easy thing to fix. Once you get your songs cleared, they can be found on www.ascap.com, www.sesac.com and/ or, www.bmi.com. This is useful because if someone has heard your song on the radio or somewhere else and wants to use it in a film, TV show, or advertisement, she will be able to find you in order to contact you and obtain a license. In fact, the most common place for a potential licenser to look for the correct contact on a given song is on the applicable performing right society website.

Once the PRO gauntlet has been negotiated (actually, it is really easy), you can concentrate on making your music and waiting for your money to come in. Remember, though, that the performing right societies are typically nine months behind in their payments. So if your song was played on the Rose Bowl telecast on January 2, don't be hounding your performing right society for your royalties until after the start of the next year, when the royalties for the first quarter (ended March 31) are actually paid.

Once you get the hang of it, clearing new songs as you write and release them is no big deal.

SCUMBAG RECORD COMPANIES

The next step is to issue a mechanical license to the record company. If the record company happens to be you (or your group), then you might not want to go through all the hassle of having your publishing company issue a license to your record company, and then paying royalties back to yourself. If, on the other hand, the record label is a bona fide third party, you will have to issue a mechanical license to ensure that you are paid your publishing income. This can be the trickiest part.

First, you have to figure out the rate at which you should be licensing. You will have to read the applicable controlled composition clause, and calculate out how much you are supposed to be paid for each copy sold. Reread the "Controlled Composition Clauses" chapter for help on how to do this. You might need your lawyer to help you with the contractual interpretation and calculation. Likewise, you might need help in obtaining an appropriate blank form of mechanical license. Reread the "Mechanical Licenses" chapter for a refresher on the potential pitfalls. Do not sign a license form that the record company has sent to you. A mechanical license form is *not* just a mechanical license form. There is a huge amount of variation from one form to another as to what the licenses do, and how and when the royalties are paid. It is really important that you make sure you are getting paid in the manner you are supposed to. Filling out the form is the easiest part. Getting the right form, appropriate to your situation, is the toughest. Once you have done this, you can use this form for all songs on your album, and future albums, subject to appropriate song, timing, and rate adjustments.

If your record is being released in Canada, you will want to issue a mechanical license directly to the Canadian record company, or else use CMRRA to do so on your behalf.

FOURTH BASE

The big three steps covered above—copyright, clearance, and mechanical licensing—pretty well cover most of the easy things that you can do yourself without too much difficulty.

There are additional things you can do, although you may or may not find them to be cost-effective uses of your time, depending on your point of view and your current level of success.

If your record is going to be released throughout the world, it is important to arrange for foreign collection of your earnings. The best DIY way to do this is to find someone to do your foreign collections and administration outside of the U.S. and Canada. ASCAP, BMI, and SESAC will effectively collect your foreign performing right earnings, so no need to worry there. But your mechanical and other types of income are best collected by someone with offices or subpublishers in the territory. A single foreign collection agent would be your best choice at this point. The hassle of having separate deals for each territory or territorial grouping is best left to those with strong stomachs, good negotiation skills, and plenty of time on their hands. Setting up 20 different deals with good subpublishers, and doing all the necessary tax exemption/reduction forms for each territory, is a job best handled by those wanting to be full-fledged music publishing companies and not just a band handling its own publishing matters.

It may be hard to find someone competent to do this for you, especially at a new band level, because as discussed above, it may well cost someone more money to collect your income than he will earn from doing the work. Many companies that are willing to do this for new publishers take a big fee and don't really pay any attention to you—they just throw your songs into the machinery and see if anyone sends them any money to send you. Make sure that these sorts of deals have a finite end date not too far in the future where ALL the rights you granted them expire. There are a few plan Bs, such as direct collection with foreign societies. You may not be able to collect all types of income this way (synchronization uses, for example), but your choice may come down to collecting something versus collecting nothing.

In addition to copyright, clearance, and mechanical licensing, you can probably do some initial and simple licensing yourself. This might include synchronization uses, ringtones, karaoke, sheet music, and other sundry uses. If the phone rings because someone has tracked you down through the ASCAP website and wants to use your song on *Pimp My Car,* you can probably muddle through the negotiation and licensing yourself, or with the help of someone more knowledgeable than yourself in sync licensing (such as your lawyer or record company). Be cautious, too, in not signing license forms people submit to you for signature without appropriate review by those well-experienced in such matters. Al and Bob Kohn's book, *Kohn on Music Licensing,* has some workable general forms as well.

If warranted by expected income, you can also join CMRRA to collect non-mechanical income types such as blank-tape levies and broadcast mechanicals. You might also try to negotiate and prepare co-writer, co-publishing, and co-administration deals. But most of these things are really not warranted at the new band level and require specialized skills and knowledge that takes years to acquire.

When Steven Spielberg's people call and want to make your song the opening theme of *Jaws VIII,* or if you are getting weekly license requests that you somehow muddle through, you are probably now out of your negotiation league and most likely better off handing the ball off to someone else. At this stage, many publishers and administrators will be interested in working with you, as you have graduated beyond the DIY stage and your time is better spent on creative matters. That is, unless you have enjoyed your brief but fruitful career as a music publisher and decide to chuck the songwriting in favor of the long-term benefits of a highly lucrative career in the music publishing field.

APPENDIX:
CAN YOU DO THE SPLITS?

The process of splitting publishing money is often very confusing, especially because the splits for performing income and other types of income are not the same. For example, a writer might receive 45% of a publisher's performing right receipts and 67.5% of a publisher's mechanical right receipts.

To help you understand how splits typically work, here are a series of common scenarios that get progressively more complex. For novices (and even non-novices), it is often useful to make diagrams with summaries at the end, as I have done here. These examples show the ultimate disposition of $100 in earnings, but can also be viewed as showing how 100% of income is split.

1. John is a 100% writer and Stinky Songs is the 100% publisher.

SUMMARY

Performance income:

Performing right society pays $50 to John as writer share.

Performing right society pays $50 to Stinky as publisher share.

Other income:

Source pays Stinky $100. Stinky pays John $50, or 50%, as writer share.

Thus Stinky pays none of its performing right receipts to John, and 50% of all other receipts to him.

2. John and Bill are each 50% writers and Stinky Songs is the 100% publisher.

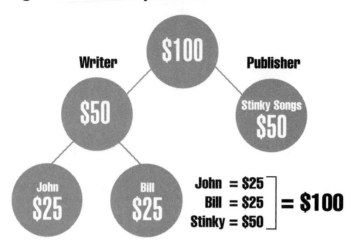

SUMMARY

Performance income:

Performing right society pays $25 to John as writer share and $25 to Bill as writer share.

Performing right society pays $50 to Stinky as publisher share.

Other income:

Source pays Stinky $100. Stinky pays $25 (25/100, or 25%) each to John and Bill as writer shares. Stinky retains $50, or 50%.

Thus Stinky pays none of its performing right receipts to any writer, and 25% of other receipts to John and 25% to Bill.

3. John is the sole writer and has a 50%/50% co-publishing deal with Stinky Songs.

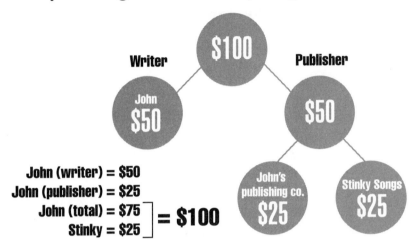

John (writer) = $50
John (publisher) = $25
John (total) = $75
Stinky = $25] = $100

SUMMARY

Performance income:

Performing right society pays John $50 as writer share.
Performing right society pays Stinky $50, which pays John 50%, or $25, and retains the same amount.

Other income:

Source pays Stinky $100. Stinky pays John $50 as writer (50/100, or 50%) and $25 as publisher (25/100, or 25%) while retaining $25 (25/100, or 25%).

Thus Stinky pays John 50% of performing income and 75% (50% + 25%) of other income.

4. John is the sole writer and has a 50%/50% co-publishing deal with Stinky Songs, which gets a 10% administration fee off the top.

Mechanical Synchronization and Non-performance Income

John (writer) = $45.00
John (publisher) = $22.50
Stinky (admin.) = $10.00
Stinky (publisher) = $22.50

John (total) = $67.50
Stinky (total) = $32.50 ⎤ = $100

PUBLIC PERFORMANCE

John (writer) = $50.00
John (publisher) = $22.50
Stinky (admin.) = $5.00
Stinky (publisher) = $22.50

John (total) = $72.50
Stinky (total) = $27.50 $\Bigg] = \$100$

Paid by the performing right society to the writer and, in this example, to Stinky, which administers 100% of the song. We are assuming that there is no contractual right to double the administration fee on the publisher's share of performance income.

SUMMARY

Performance income:

Performing right society pays John $50 as writer share.

Performing right society pays $50 to Stinky. Stinky then pays $22.50 to John's publishing company (22.50/50, or 45%), retains an administration fee of $5 (5/50, or 10%), and retains $22.50 (22.50/50, or 45%) as its publisher. Note that 45% + 45% + 10% = 100%.

Other income:

Source pays $100 to Stinky. Stinky pays $45 to John as writer (45/100, or 45%) and $22.50 as publisher (22.50/100, or 22.5%), or $67.50 (67.5%) total, while retaining $32.50 (32.50/100, or 32.5%).

Thus Stinky pays John 45% of performing income and 67.5% of all other income.

5. John is the sole writer and has a 75%/25% co-publishing deal (in his favor) with Stinky Songs.

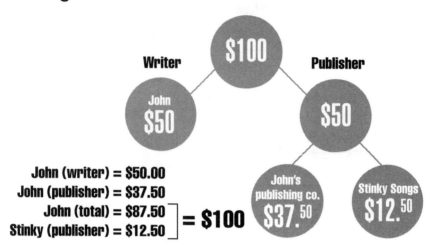

John (writer) = $50.00
John (publisher) = $37.50
John (total) = $87.50
Stinky (publisher) = $12.50
⎤ = $100

SUMMARY

Performance income:

Performing right society pays John $50 as writer share.

Performing right society pays Stinky $50 as the 100% administering publishing company. Stinky then pays John's publishing company $37.50 (37.50/50, or 75%) and retains the remaining $12.50 (12.50/50, or 25%).

Other income:

Source pays $100 to Stinky. Stinky pays $50 to John as writer (50/100, or 50%) and $37.50 as publisher (37.50/100, or 37.5%), or $87.50 (87.5%) total, while retaining $12.50 (12.5%).

Thus Stinky pays John 75% of performing income and 87.5% of all other income.

6. John and Bill are each 50% writers. John kept his publisher share, but Bill has a 50%/50% co-publishing deal with Stinky Songs.

John (writer) = $25.00
John (publisher) = $25.00
Bill (writer) = $25.00
Bill (publisher) = $12.50

John (total) = $50.00
Bill (total) = $37.50 } = **$100**
Stinky = $12.50

SUMMARY

Performance income:

Performing right society pays $25 to John as writer share and $25 to Bill as writer share.

Performing right society pays John's publishing company $25.

Performing right society pays Stinky $25. Stinky then pays $12.50 (12.50/25, or 50%) to Bill's publishing company while retaining $12.50 (12.50/25, or 50%).

Other income:

Source pays John's publishing company $50. John (as the publisher) sends half to himself as songwriter (he really doesn't have to do this) and retains the rest as publisher share.

Source pays Stinky $50. Stinky pays Bill $25 (25/50, or 50%) as his writer share plus $12.50 (12.5/50, or 25%) as his publisher share. Stinky retains $12.50 (12.5/50, or 25%). Note that Stinky pays Bill a total of $37.50 (or 75% of its receipts) and retains $12.50 (or 25% of its receipts).

7. John wrote 80% of the song and Bill wrote 20% of the song. They agreed to give half of the publishing money to the film company that was using it as a major motion picture opening title song. Of the remaining half of the publishing, John had a 50%/50% co-publishing deal with Stinky Songs, and Bill had a 75%/25% co-publishing deal (in his favor) with Stinky Songs.

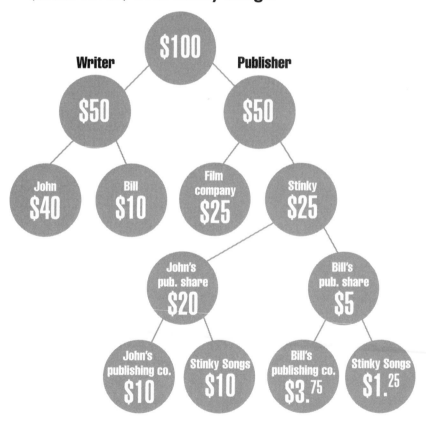

John (writer) = $40.00	John (total) = $50.00
John (publisher) = $10.00	Bill (total) = $13.75
Bill (writer) = $10.00	Film company = $25.00
Bill (publisher) = $3.75	Stinky = $11.25

$$= \$100$$

SUMMARY

Performance income:

Performing right society pays John $40 (80% of $50) and Bill $10 (20% of $50) as writer shares.

Performing right society pays film company $25, or 50% of the publisher share.

Performing right society pays Stinky $25, which pays $10 to John's publishing company (10/25, or 40% of receipts) and $3.75 to Bill's publishing company (3.75/25, or 15%) while retaining $11.25 (11.25/25, or 45%).

Other income:

Film company collects $25 (we assume that the contract is such that the film company does not collect any writer share of income).

Stinky collects $75 and pays John $40 (40/75, or 53.3%) as writer, and $10 (10/75, or 13.3%) as publisher. Stinky pays Bill $10 (10/75, or 13.3%) as writer, and $3.75 (3.75/75, or 5%) as publisher. Stinky retains $11.25 (11.25/75, or 15%). Note that 53.3% + 13.3% + 13.3% + 5% + 15% = 100% of Stinky's receipts.

GLOSSARY

360 deal A deal that covers not only recording services but a full range of professional services. A 360 deal might cover recording services, live performances, merchandising rights, publishing rights, and other professional services.

Access model A consumer music delivery service that is based upon having access to electronic music files as opposed to actually owning a physical product (such as a CD). Pandora is an access model service. Access models may include a monthly fee or be supported by advertising, etc.

Ad card A credit notice within an advertising use, often in smaller type at the bottom of the screen identifying the name of the song and the group. Also called a chyron. Ad cards are often given for promotional value to compensate for a lower-than-normal fee.

Ad supported A method of music delivery that has no cost to the end consumer and for which the service obtains its operating and profit revenue through the sale of advertising. YouTube is an ad-supported service.

Administration The handling of all the day-to-day functions of a music publisher, such as (but not limited to) registering copyrights, clearing songs with performing right societies, negotiating and issuing licenses, collecting and reviewing royalties, and accounting and paying out royalties to writers, publishers, and other authorized participants. In an "administration deal," the administrator does not take ownership equity in copyrights, as opposed to a "co-publishing deal" where ownership in the copyright is given to the company that is also doing the administration.

Aggregate mechanical cap To limit their maximum liability for mechanical royalties on a given album, record companies get artists to agree that the company will not be liable for royalties that exceed the amount earned by a given number of songs, or otherwise a fixed amount in dollars and cents. For instance, if you and the record company agreed to an aggregate mechanical cap of "12 songs at the minimum statutory rate at the date of initial release," then the record company is protected against your turning in an album with 52 songs on it (each 15 seconds long) and having to pay you 52 times the statutory rate.

Artist royalty What the record company pays you to be a recording artist (i.e., as a musician or singer). Sometimes called a recording royalty. This does not relate to your songwriting or composing, which is covered separately by the payment of mechanical royalties.

Black box income In many territories, the performing or mechanical right societies put all of the uncollected and/or unallocable income earned in their territories into a so-called black box account. This money is alternatively referred to as copyright control or suspense income. When copyright control or suspense income remains unclaimed for a specified (but varying by territory) period of time, the money "goes black box" and is then divided up among everyone else who earned money from that source. It's like dividing up extra spoils.

Blanket license A license for an entire repertoire, instead of licensing on a song-by-song basis. For example, a TV station obtaining a blanket license from ASCAP gets to publicly perform every song in the ASCAP repertoire, and doesn't have to ask for permission to perform a given ASCAP song each time.

Bonus records *See* Free goods.

Broad rights license A comprehensive license form that covers just about everything the licenser can think of. This is opposed to a specific, limited license. For example, a broad rights synchronization license might cover TV, in-context advertising, motion picture theatrical rights, and home video devices. A TV sync license would only cover TV broadcast.

Bump A performance or milestone bonus. A low-budget synchronization license might have bumps specifying additional payments to the publisher when a film attains box office receipts of $5 million, $10 million, etc. A deal that has bumps is referred to as a step deal. *See* step deal.

Buyout A deal based not upon a royalty per unit but upon a fixed agreed fee. A buyout license can be for the life of a song's copyright (plus renewals and extensions, if any) or for a fixed period of time. For example, you can grant someone a five-year video buyout in which he can use your song on as many concert DVD videos as he can sell within that term.

Catalog An aggregation or collection of musical songs. For example, the Sea of Tunes catalog includes most of the big hit songs written by Brian Wilson and the Beach Boys.

Central licensing A European mechanical licensing model whereby records are manufactured in a single country within the European Union. For example, Universal Music might elect to manufacture and centrally license all of its CDs in the Netherlands, rather than duplicating function and effort by manufacturing in the Netherlands, Germany, France, Italy, Spain, England, etc. Centrally licensed and paid mechanical royalties are then paid out by the central licenser to each society within each European Union country in which the records are ultimately distributed.

Chyron *See* Ad card.

Circular A pamphlet on a given topic.

Co-administration agreement An agreement between writers and/or publishers that specifies the writer and publisher shares, and who is responsible for the administration of the work.

Compulsory license Generally, a license that is automatic and for which a publisher's explicit permission is not needed. With respect to phonorecords, this is a license that a record company obtains automatically as long as it complies with the compulsory license provisions of the copyright law.

Common Works Registration (CWR) A standard format for the registration and revision of song data. CWR includes the data necessary for a Publisher to register a work at a Performing or Mechanical Rights Society.

Consent Decree In legal speak, it is a voluntary agreement between parties to withdraw or stay a lawsuit and instead operate under court approved terms or supervision. With respect to music publishing, so as to not run afoul of antitrust regulations and monopolistic behaviors, both ASCAP and BMI operate under consent decrees under which a federal judge determines what they can or cannot do. The consent decrees in effect for ASCAP and BMI have tied their hands with respect to free and open market negotiations for their music performing rights and rates, which are instead determined by the courts and not a negotiation by the parties. SESAC does not operate under a consent decree.

Controlled Refers to a writer, publisher, or song that is subject to a controlled composition clause.

Controlled composition clause A clause (often very long and specific) within a recording agreement that specifies an agreement between the recording artist and the record company for songs that the artist writes, co-writes, and/or desires to record. In general, the controlled composition clause greatly cuts back on the liabilities and costs to the record company for mechanical royalties compared to what it would otherwise have had to pay under copyright law.

Co-publishing An arrangement in which one or more writers or publishers have a stake in a given work. In a co-publishing deal, a writer typically assigns half of his copyrights to a music publishing company in exchange for monetary or other benefits. A co-publishing deal may also be described as selling half of your publishing ownership and usually all of your administration rights.

Copyright Ownership of intellectual property such as songs, software, books, and paintings, and the legal rights granted in connection with that ownership.

Copyright royalty Usually (in the context of this book) refers to the fees to be paid for the use of a composition, as opposed to the fees to be paid as artist royalties.

Copyright control *See* Black box income.

Copyright Royalty Board Consists of three Copyright Royalty Judges who determine the rates and terms of statutory licenses. The judges are appointed by the Librarian of Congress. The constitutionality of how judges are appointed to the Copyright Royalty Board has been challenged by those who don't like the rates which have been set, but as of May 2013, the Supreme Court has refused to hear an appeal challenging that process, and the board remains intact and with authority.

CRB *See* Copyright Royalty Board.

Cue sheet An (often multipage) listing of all the songs appearing in a given film or TV show, showing all the music titles incorporated within the work, including other information such as the composers, the publishers, the type of use, the length of use, shares of ownership, etc. Performing right societies use cue sheets to determine who is to be paid for the performance of the music when a film or TV show that includes the music is publicly performed. It is crucial that publishers/writers verify the information listed on the cue sheet for any film or TV show that uses their music, and ensure that the appropriate performing right societies have received the cue sheet.

CWR *See* Common Works Registration.

Derivative work A work that is based upon or incorporates elements of a previously copyrighted work. Sampling or the creation of a medley may result in a derivative work. In general, permission of the owner of material incorporated into a derivative work is required under strict penalty of law. An unauthorized derivative work is an infringement, or a violation, of copyright law. If willful or intentional (as opposed to "accidental"), this unauthorized use is a felony.

Digital phonograph delivery (DPD) Delivery of a master recording by electronic means, such as via the Internet. Often this is in the form of an MP3 format electronic file. This is different from when you buy a physical product at a record store, but for mechanical licensing and royalty purposes, DPDs are usually treated the same as physical phonorecords.

Digital song file *See* Digital phonograph delivery.

Direct performance license A license used when someone who will publicly perform copyrighted works (whether or not for profit) negotiates a license directly with the copyright owner (the publisher) instead of with a performing right society. Songwriter/publisher agreements with most performing right societies permit affiliated publishers to directly license works for performance to end users as long as they notify the societies.

DPD *See* Digital phonograph delivery.

eCO An online copyright registration system through www.copyright.gov (electronic Copyright Office).

Employee for hire The creator of a work for hire. *See* Work for hire.

Employer for hire The party that commissions a work for hire. *See* Work for hire.

Ephemeral use A transitory, non-permanent use of a work. A typical example is a TV broadcast of a marching band in a parade performing a copyrighted song. The broadcaster had no way of knowing the song would be performed or broadcast and is generally not held liable for failing to pre-license this ephemeral synchronized use.

Exclusive A type of agreement or use whereby all other parties are precluded from making a similar use. An exclusive advertising license with Coca-Cola gives Coca-Cola the sole right to use your song in commercials. A non-exclusive synchronization license to use your song in *Rocky 37* allows you to license your song to other films.

Fair use Types of uses for which no license or permission is needed. Fair uses, for example, may be for educational, critical, or other free speech purposes.

Film festival license Generally a limited, short-term, theatrical license, whereby a song can be synchronized in a film for a low fee and publicly performed in film competitions and the like. A publisher is under no obligation to grant or permit a film festival license.

Fix The process of recording the details of a composition in a tangible media. Examples would be writing down a song as sheet music or recording it onto a cassette or hard drive.

Fixed medium The medium in which a work has been fixed: for example, sheet music, a cassette, or a hard drive.

Free goods Records that are (in theory) given to stores to entice them to order large quantities of records. A typical free good offer might be, "If you order 85 records, we'll send you 100." Stores also sometimes can get bonus copies to sell under other various promotional schemes.

In-context use Use of a song apart from the work in which it was originally included that maintains the same linear synchronization that it had within the original work. For example, if your song is shown over three scenes of a birthday party in a film, and then those three scenes are aired on TV when an actor appears on Letterman to promote the film, and your music is used in the exact same manner as it was in the film, the use is in-context. An example of an *out-of-context* use is if your song from that film is used as a musical bed for a commercial advertising the film in which many scenes (but not the three that the song was originally synchronized with) are shown. It is typical (but not required) in a broad rights synchronization license to give in-context promotional uses, but to reserve (and thus license separately for an additional fee) out-of-context uses.

Joint work A work created by two or more authors who intend their individual contributions to be merged into a new whole work. A newly co-written song is a joint work. A famous poem set to music is a derivative work.

Lean back A type of streaming service which is not interactive, and where the musical material provided is not directly controlled by the listener, but rather broadcast and determined by the service. The alternative would be an "on-demand" service where the listener picks what he hears.

Linear Used to describe a non-variable, one-to-one correspondence of sound and picture. Used when describing in-context uses. *See* in-context use

Long-song rate U.S. copyright law specifies additional statutory mechanical payments for songs greater than 5 minutes in length. If the performance runs longer, you get paid more.

Master license The license of a particular artist's recorded performance. A master license does not include the right to use the underlying musical composition, which must be licensed separately from the publisher (copyright owner).

Mechanical license The license to use a song for phonorecords. This is for the right to use a composition, not for the right to use a given master recording (which is covered by the master license). Mechanical licenses are audio only, and do not cover synchronized uses with pictures as in films, TV programs, or videos.

Mechanical royalty The royalty payable to the publisher (owner of the song) for a mechanical license. Usually specified in the United States as so many cents per copy made and distributed (even if not sold).

Mechanical royalty pool The royalty pool established by a record company in conjunction with an aggregate mechanical cap. For example, a record company might negotiate a contract with a recording artist whereby the record company funds a mechanical royalty pool of $1 per album in connection with an aggregate mechanical cap. This $1 per album would first be allocated to the publishers of non-controlled songs, and then the remaining pool would be spent on all the remaining controlled songs. *See also* Aggregate mechanical cap, Controlled.

MFN *See* Most favored nations.

Min-max A type of controlled composition clause in which the record company is assured of a maximum aggregate mechanical payout and thus has its costs contained, and the artist (publisher in this case) has correspondingly gotten the record company to agree that if the aggregate mechanical costs are less than it agreed to pay, he receives the difference as a minimum. For example, if a record company has agreed to pay for ten songs per album on a "min-max" basis and the artist/writer puts 12 songs on the record, each song is paid at 10/12 of the agreed rate. On the other hand, if the artist/writer puts only eight songs on the record, he is paid 10/8 of the agreed rate for each song. In effect the artist says to the record company, "I'll help you contain your costs, but if there's extra left over from your budget, I get it."

Monetization The process whereby income is derived by driving traffic to a website or page. For example, monetization results when a recording artist puts a video onto YouTube, and for which YouTube either sells pre-roll or static advertisements shown to the viewer either before, during, or after the view. The advertising revenue, which shared with the artist or song publisher, is referred to as monetization insofar as income is derived from each public viewing.

Moral rights Per the Berne Convention, "Independently of the author's economic rights, and even after the transfer of the said rights, the author shall have the right to claim authorship of the work and to object to any distortion, mutilation or other modification of, or other derogatory action in relation to, the said work, which would be prejudicial to his honor or reputation." In plain English, moral rights mean that even if you sell your work, you still have certain rights that survive the sale. The buyer cannot distort, mutilate, or modify the art you have created just because he owns it. Moral rights are troublesome, for example, to film studios, which want the right to distort and modify a director's or editor's work for such things as editing length or content for TV showings. Countries that are signatory to the Berne Convention afford their creators moral rights and greater protection of their art and reputation than non-signatory countries.

Most favored nations (MFN) A clause in a contract assuring that no other contracting or licensing party is being treated more favorably or with better material terms. For example, if you license your song to a video project for "10¢ per unit sold on an MFN basis," and then the licenser agrees to pay the Rolling Stones 14¢ per unit sold, you are guaranteed to get the same rate the Rolling Stones got, which is the highest rate the producer is paying.

Music publishing Generally, the ownership of the rights to a musical composition (and not the printing of sheet music).

Name, image, and likeness (NIL) The right, separate and apart from the use of a composition, to use the author's name, image, signature, or likeness in conjunction with a product. For example, a sheet music company that has licensed the right to use your songs in a songbook might also want to license NIL rights so it can use a photograph of you on the cover of the book.

Negative pickup A film deal in which the film is made independently, and then a studio or distributer obtains (picks up) the right from the original producer to distribute the film (the finished negative).

Net publisher share The amount a publisher retains after paying all third party royalties, such as songwriter and any publisher participant royalties. This is like net profit for the music publisher.

NIL *See* Name, image, and likeness.

NOI *See* Notice of intent.

Non-controlled Not subject to a controlled composition clause. Usually a non-controlled writer/publisher is a co-writer who is not part of the recording artist, or is the publisher of an outside song such as a cover recording. *See* controlled composition clause

Non-exclusive Not exclusive. *See also* Exclusive.

Non-surveyed performances Public performances that are not monitored by performing right societies. For example, the ABC television network is monitored, and the results of the monitoring are used to allocate and distribute money that organizations like ASCAP collect. Non-surveyed performances are at places like Mo's Bar on the corner. Your song might be played a lot at Mo's, and Mo might have an ASCAP license, but ASCAP isn't monitoring (surveying) performances at Mo's to see who it (ASCAP) should pay.

Notice of Intent (NOI) A legal notice that must be served upon a publisher 30 days prior to distribution of phonorecords. If a correct and legal notice is not served, the would-be user is precluded from subsequently obtaining a compulsory license. In many cases, record companies intend their NOI to serve as a mechanical license request as opposed to actually complying with compulsory license requirements.

On-demand A type of streaming service which is interactive, and where the musical material provided is directly controlled by the listener. The alternative would be a "lean back" service where the service picks what is played for the listener.

Out-of-context use Use taken out of context from its original synchronization. *See also* In-context use.

PA and PAu copyrights Copyrights for the performing arts. PA copyrights cover songs as well as dramatic works, scripts, pantomimes, choreography, motion pictures, and other audiovisual works. PAu is the designation given to unpublished (not yet publicly distributed) works of the performing arts.

Pan-European Licensing A central licensing program (see "Central Licensing") operating within Europe so as to cover all European countries.

Parody lyrics In music publishing vernacular, parody lyrics are not necessarily lyrics that humorously mock the originals, but may be lyrics rewritten to fit the situation. For example, changing the line "Sweet little rock 'n' roller" to "Boy, I like Coca-Cola" would be considered creating a parody lyric. Parody lyrics in this sense must be approved by the original publisher and almost always command a premium over a licensed non-parody use. A true parody use may also be a fair use.

Penny rate A royalty rate fixed in dollars and cents, rather than expressed in a percentage. For example, in relative terms, you might get 14% of the suggested retail selling price. In penny rate terms, your agreement might state that you get a flat $2.25 per CD sold. U.S. statutory mechanical rates are fixed as penny rates (currently 9.1¢ if the song is under 5 minutes in length) while foreign mechanical rates are often expressed as percentages.

Perfecting the rights When a music licensee returns to license additionally needed or desired rights. For example, a licensee may have TV rights and Home Video rights, but may not have contemplated the future existence of streaming rights, and now therefore wishes to acquire them. Typically, someone looking to perfect their rights will seek to expand their previously licensed rights to include all possible uses "now known or hereinafter devised" and will pay an additional fee to do so.

Performance royalty A royalty paid for the public performance of a copyrighted work. In most instances, performance royalties are paid by a performing right society but may be negotiated and paid directly between the user and publisher. Performance royalties are split into writer shares (50%) and publisher shares (50%) by the performing right societies.

Performing right society Organizations that license public performances on behalf of music publishers, and then pay them royalties for the licensed performances. In the United States, the main performing right organizations in order of decreasing size are ASCAP, BMI, and SESAC. Most performing right societies throughout the world are either nonprofit corporations (in the U.S., operating under consent decree court supervision) or government controlled.

Per-program license In lieu of getting a blanket license to publicly perform a performing right society's entire repertoire, some users of music opt to pay on a per-use basis. With a per-program license, they apply and pay for a public performance license to use only the music embodied in their programs.

Phonorecord According to the United States copyright law, "material objects in which sounds, other than those accompanying a motion picture or other audiovisual work, are fixed by any method now known or later developed, and from which the sounds can be perceived, reproduced, or otherwise communicated, either directly or with the aid of a machine or device."

Physical Refers to a music delivery good that is tangible and owned by the purchaser, such as a compact disc or vinyl phonograph record, as opposed to an electronic music file (DPD) which has no physical form. Also, an insipid pop record from 1981 by Olivia Newton-John that no one could get out of their head until 1983.

Preferred price to dealers (PPD) A term used mostly in Europe to describe an amount to which a royalty rate is applied. PPD is somewhat arbitrary but is closely akin to the wholesale selling price paid by a majority of retailers for a product. Mechanical rates per album in many European countries are 9.09% of PPD.

Premium content Material uploaded to YouTube by a label or company for the explicit purpose of making money via advertising monetization, as opposed to "user generated," which is uploaded by an individual without a profit motive.

Prima facie Evidence in a case or claim that is sufficient to establish it as truth in the absence of further facts or proof, such as a copyright certificate.

Professional manager A music publisher's employee whose job it is to attempt to secure desirable licensing activity for the publisher's songs. Professional managers contact and visit record producers, film music supervisors, advertising agencies, etc., and try to convince them to use the publisher's songs. An older term is song plugger.

Promotional records Records given away for promotional purposes. In general, artists and publishers are not paid for promotional records, which are usually marked "not for sale" and drilled or cosmetically disfigured to prevent them from being sold as new product. Promotional records are different from free goods, which are intended to be sold. *See also* Free goods.

Publisher half Traditionally, the writer and the publisher have split all income on a 50%/50% basis. These roles have changed and in most cases today the writer is also the publisher, but the concept of splitting all publishing income into writer and publisher halves has persisted.

Recording royalty *See* Artist royalty.

Recoupable Describes any money advanced to you or on your behalf that will be recovered from your future earnings. Typical recoupable costs to a recording artist are advances, recording costs, video costs, equipment funds, producer fees, etc., which are recouped against your artist royalties. Publishing income (including mechanical royalties) is not recoupable against anything unless you have specifically agreed that it will be.

Rest of world (ROW) Publishing deals often carve out certain territories, and what is left after the carving is the ROW. For example, if you self-administer your publishing rights for the United States and Canada but plan to hire someone to administer and collect elsewhere, you are seeking a ROW deal.

Rights There are many different and highly specific types of licenses a publisher may agree to. These licenses cover different rights, such as the right to synchronize, publicly perform, make phonorecords, or create advertisements using a given song.

Right holders Synonymous with copyright owner. Within the context of this book, right holders are music publishers (with respect to owning the copyrights to songs) and record companies (with respect to owning master recordings).

Ringtone An electronic song or sequence of notes that plays when a cell phone is called. The licensing of songs by music publishers for ringtones now generates more than $3 billion per year throughout the world. Ringtones may be monophonic (a single-tone melody), polyphonic (chords and melody), and "tru-tones" (actual master recordings, such as the Doors' "Hello I Love You"), and may or may not be combined with special graphics or screen animation.

Safe harbor Refers to a legal defense whereby if a party complies with certain legal formalities, they cannot be sued under law. Specifically in music publishing, it usually refers to the ability of a service such as YouTube to be exempt from legal liability in the case where they themselves did not upload infringing material, but instead where the infringing material was "user uploaded." YouTube would then be able to avail itself of a safe harbor defense ("It wasn't me.")

Sampling The use of other copyrighted material to create a new work. Samples may be of compositions and/or master recordings, and may be authorized or unauthorized (in which case the sample constitutes copyright infringement).

Song plugger *See* Professional manager

Songwriting deal A business deal that pays you to write songs for the additional benefit of a third party. There are many types of songwriting deals, such as agreements in which a publisher owns your songs and pays you a royalty, co-publishing deals (where you are partners of sorts), and work-for-hire agreements.

Split Shorthand for how money or ownership is divided. A "50%/50% split on writing" means that you are a half writer and your partner is a half writer. Splits can be quite complex.

SR copyright A sound recording copyright; that is, a copyright in the audio recording of a specific performance. This is the copyright for a master recording and does not necessarily cover the copyright in the underlying composition, which may be owned by a third party. *See also* PA copyright.

Statutory rate The U.S. mechanical rate for the reproduction of a composition on phonorecords as determined by law (or statute). Current (beginning in 2004) United States copyright law specifies a statutory rate for a song less than 5 minutes in length of 9.1¢ for each copy manufactured and distributed. In October 2008, a 1.5% monthly late fee was added to the 9.1¢ rate, as well as a 24¢ statutory rate for ringtones.

Step deal A synchronization deal that involves bumps, or additional back-end payments predicated upon certain levels or milestones to be reached by the licenser. *See* Bump.

Streaming A method of listening to music or watching audio-visual material over the internet without actually owning a physical copy of the material. Streaming may be on-demand (they stream what you tell them you want to hear or watch) or lean-back (they play for you what they want to play for you).

Subpublisher A third party licensee who acts in the place and stead of the original publisher within a foreign territory. Most subpublishing deals have detailed specifications and terms that limit what a subpublisher can or cannot do without the original publisher's permission. Terms of subpublishing deals vary substantially as to how the subpublisher is compensated, the length of time of the agreement, and other significant terms. These days subpublishers provide services but do not obtain an ownership interest, although foreign ownership rights were sometimes transferred in very old subpublishing deals.

Subscription service A music service that involves payment by an individual to have access to copyright material via internet streaming. For example, Rhapsody is an on-demand subscription service whereby the user pays a monthly fee (currently $9.99 per month for the basic service) and gets to listen to as much music as he wants from millions of songs without any advertising.

Suspense income Income that is held (usually by a performing or mechanical right society) pending a determination as to who is entitled to claim it. Unclaimed suspense income will become black box money after a period of time that varies by territory. *See* Black box income.

Sync agent Someone who is hired specifically to secure new synchronization licensing activity for a writer's or publisher's songs. Sync agents contact directors, film and TV music supervisors, advertising agencies, etc., and try to convince them to license the songs they represent.

Synchronization or sync license A license relating to the synchronization of a musical composition in fixed timed relation with video images. Example: the use of a song in a film or TV program.

Synchronization royalty The royalty paid for a synchronization license. In many cases, a synchronization use is paid by a flat fee covering a given set of rights for a fixed period of time. In some cases, there may be a royalty. An example of a synchronization royalty is the use of a song in a concert DVD video that is payable based on the number of units sold. *See also* Video buyout.

Tangible medium Some sort of medium upon which information may be stored, such as paper, tape, or computer hard drives. In order to qualify for a copyright, a song must be fixed in a tangible medium from which it can be subsequently reproduced.

Terrestrial or **Terrestrial** Radio Traditional radio whereby an over-the-air signal is publicly broadcast and may be received by anyone having an appropriate device. This is as opposed to so-called internet or satellite radio which is privately transmitted over non-broadcast airwaves.

User generated Material which is uploaded by an individual to YouTube (or other similar site) without a direct profit motive, as opposed to "premium content" which is uploaded with the direct intent of monetizing the material consumed.

Video buyout A fixed fee license for video synchronization. The opposite of a royalty-based deal. *See also* Buyout.

Video mechanical A term sometimes applied to royalty-based deals (as opposed to a flat-fee video buyout) covering synchronization royalties for home video devices. The video mechanical may be based upon a percentage of something (such as the video selling price) or more typically as a penny rate per unit distributed.

Work for hire A work created under the scope of employment in which the creating author is compensated but is not considered either the legal owner or author. In a work-for-hire situation (and in the rather restricted copyright type that results from it) the commissioning (or hiring) party is the legal author and owner. If you write a work for hire for Coca-Cola to be used as a new jingle, the company is legally the owner and writer of the song, and other than your fee (and whatever other consideration Coke agreed to give you), you get nothing else.

Writer half Traditionally, the 50% of publishing income belonging to the writer. *See* Publisher half.

INDEX